Abraham Lincoln

Message of the President of the United States

Communicating in Answer to a Resolution of the Senate of the 26th

Ultimo

Abraham Lincoln

Message of the President of the United States
Communicating in Answer to a Resolution of the Senate of the 26th Ultimo

ISBN/EAN: 9783744762410

Printed in Europe, USA, Canada, Australia, Japan

Cover: Foto ©Suzi / pixelio.de

More available books at **www.hansebooks.com**

38TH CONGRESS, } SENATE. { Ex. Doc.
1st Session. } { No. 17.

MESSAGE

OF THE

PRESIDENT OF THE UNITED STATES,

COMMUNICATING,

In answer to a resolution of the Senate of the 26th ultimo, correspondence with the rebel authorities in relation to the exchange of prisoners.

FEBRUARY 8, 1864.—Read, referred to the Committee on Military Affairs and the Militia, and ordered to be printed.

To the Senate:

In compliance with the resolution of the Senate of the 26th ultimo, requesting "a copy of all the correspondence between the authorities of the United States and the rebel authorities on the exchange of prisoners, and the different propositions connected with that subject," I transmit herewith a report from the Secretary of War, and the papers with which it is accompanied.

ABRAHAM LINCOLN.

WASHINGTON, *February* 4, 1864.

WAR DEPARTMENT,
Washington City, February 4, 1864.

SIR: I have the honor to return herewith the resolution of the Senate of the 26th ultimo, requesting "a copy of all the correspondence between the authorities of the United States and the rebel authorities on the exchange of prisoners, and the different propositions connected with that subject," and to transmit a copy of the report of Major General Hitchcock, commissioner for exchanges, with the accompanying papers.

Very respectfully, your obedient servant,

EDWIN M. STANTON,
Secretary of War.

The PRESIDENT.

WASHINGTON CITY, D. C.,
February 4, 1864.

SIR: I have the honor to enclose a copy of "the correspondence between the authorities of the United States and the rebel authorities on the exchange of prisoners, and the different propositions connected with that subject," called for by the Senate of the United States by resolution of the 26th ultimo.

This correspondence has been furnished by General Meredith down to the period when Major General Butler entered upon duty in connexion with the subject of exchanges, and since then by General Butler himself.

I have added a copy of the instructions to General Butler on the subject, dated Fort Monroe, December 17, 1863, signed by myself, in conformity with your orders of the previous day, a copy of which is also annexed; and I have added a copy of the cartel, so frequently referred to in this correspondence.

Very respectfully, your obedient servant,
E. A. HITCHCOCK,
Major General Volunteers, Commissioner for Exchanges.

Hon. EDWIN M. STANTON,
Secretary of War.

HEADQUARTERS DEPARTMENT OF VA., SEVENTH ARMY CORPS,
Fort Monroe, Virginia, January 16, 1863.

GENERAL: I have the honor to enclose to you a copy of the Richmond Enquirer, containing Jeff. Davis's message. His determination, avowed in most insolent terms, to deliver to the several State authorities all commissioned officers of the United States that may hereafter be captured, will, I think, be persevered in. You will recollect that after the proclamation of Jeff. Davis, of the 23d of December, 1862, I urgently advised another interview, (the last one I had with Mr. Ould, and in which very important exchanges were declared;) I then did so anticipating that the cartel might be broken, and wishing to make sure of the discharge from their parole of 10,000 of our men. This was effected, and in a manner so advantageous to our government that we gained in the count of 20,000 exchanged about 7,000 men. I had almost equal good success in the exchange declared on November 11, 1862. If an open rupture should now occur in the execution of the cartel, we are all well prepared for it. I am endeavoring to get away from confederate prisons all our officers captured previously to the date of the message of Jeff. Davis, (the 12th instant,) with what success I shall know early next week.

As you may receive this copy of the message in advance of any other, may I ask that it be transmitted to the Secretary of War, or the general-in-chief, with the additional information conveyed in this communication to you.

I am, very respectfully, your obedient servant,
WILLIAM H. LUDLOW,
Lieut. Colonel and Agent for Exchange of Prisoners.

Major General HITCHCOCK,
Commissioner for the Exchange of Prisoners.

Copy of the paragraph in the message of Jefferson Davis, as published in the Richmond Enquirer, January 15, 1863, and referred to in the preceding letter.

"So far as regards the action of this government on such criminals as may attempt its execution, I confine myself to informing you that I shall, unless in your wisdom you deem some other course more expedient, deliver to the several State authorities all commissioned officers of the United States that may hereafter be captured by our forces in any of the States embraced in the proclamation, that they may be dealt with in accordance with the laws of those States providing for the punishment of criminals engaged in exciting servile insurrection.

"The enlisted soldiers I shall continue to treat as unwilling instruments in the commission of these crimes, and shall direct their discharge and return to their homes on the proper and usual parole."

RICHMOND, VIRGINIA,
January 17, 1863.

SIR: I regretted very much, on reaching City Point, meridian, on the 16th instant, to find you had left. I did not receive any notice that you would be obliged to leave at eleven o'clock on that day. If I had, however, I do not see how I could have been at City Point any sooner.

In your communication of the 14th instant you desire to know whether the federal commissioned officers now prisoners will be released. I have already furnished you with an official copy of the proclamation of President Davis, dated December 23, 1862. In conformity therewith officers will not be released on parole, but will be exchanged for those of corresponding rank. If you have any confederate officer in your possession and will deliver him, an officer of like grade will be delivered to you, and they will be mutually declared to be exchanged. So if you have released any officer on parole, we will deliver to you an officer of corresponding rank, and declare them exchanged. The federal officers, however, now in our possession, will not be surrendered to you on parole. This rule will apply only to commissioned officers. We are ready at any time to release on parole and deliver to you your non-commissioned officers and privates.

This course has been forced upon the confederate government, not only by the refusal of the authorities of the United States to respond to the repeated applications of this government in relation to the execution of Mumford, but by their persistence in retaining confederate officers who were entitled to parole and exchange. You have now of captures that are by no means recent many officers of the confederate service who are retained in your military prisons east and west. Applications have been made for the release of some without success, and others have been kept in confinement so long as to justify the conclusion that you refuse both parole and exchange.

One prominent instance I will bring to your notice: General B. F. Butler has retained Brigadier General Clarke, and thirteen others, for several months. At the latest advices received by us they were still in custody. During the whole of the time that they have been thus detained, we had a large excess of federal prisoners, all of whom were either promptly exchanged or delivered to you on parole.

This is by no means a solitary case. I have now, and have had for a long time, authentic evidence in possession of the retention of a large number of confederate officers by your military authorities. Several prominent cases have also very recently been presented to me. You are very well aware that this has been a subject of complaint ever since the adoption of the cartel. In view of all these facts, the confederate government has determined to refuse any parole to your officers until the grievances of which it has complained are redressed. Of course this applies to such commissioned officers as were captured before the date of President Davis's message. He himself has indicated what disposition will be made of such as may be captured after that date.

In your communication of the 14th instant you also refer to the case of Mrs. Piggott, who, you say, "was taken from her home at Williamsburg, Virginia, with forty of her slaves, and who is now detained at Richmond, or some other place within the confederate lines."

Without any comment upon the singularity of the request, that slaves made free by President Lincoln's proclamation should be promptly returned as the property of Mrs. Piggott, I inform you that Mrs. Piggott was released from custody on habeas corpus a long time ago. She is a citizen of Virginia, responsible to the laws of that State, and the confederacy. The confederate and State authorities will not allow any interference by the United States with the course of justice in any one of the confederate States. They will not entertain even a protest. No fears of retaliation upon "ladies," or any one else, will ever make them relinquish their rightful and exclusive control.

I perceive by your published notice of exchanges that you have made a mistake in declaring exchanged the federal prisoners paroled at Goldsboro', and delivered at Washington, North Carolina. These are the thirteen hundred that I have so constantly pressed upon you, and for whom you have given no equivalent or credit. You have the list in your possession. I delivered it to you that you might examine more fully into the matter. Those men have not been exchanged. I hope you will make the proper correction.

When shall I see you at City Point again?

Respectfully, your obedient servant,

ROBERT OULD,
Agent of Exchange.

Lieut. Colonel LUDLOW,
Agent of Exchange.

CITY POINT, VIRGINIA, *January* 14, 1863.

SIR: May I have the pleasure of an early as possible interview with you. I desire to know whether, in compliance with the terms of the cartel, the commissioned United States officers now in your hands are to be released, and also what disposition has been made of the case of Mrs. Piggott, who was taken from her home at Williamsburg, Va., with forty of her slaves, and who is now detained at Richmond or some other place within the confederate lines.

Major General Dix, some time since, communicated with you on this case.

He has received pressing applications to retaliate by the arrest and imprisonment of ladies within our lines, whose avowed sentiments and conduct have been persistently disloyal to the United States government. Can you not have this matter arranged by the prompt return of Mrs. Piggott and all her property to her home.

I am, very respectfully, your obedient servant,

WM. H. LUDLOW,
Lieutenant Colonel and Agent for Exchange of Prisoners.

Hon. ROBERT OULD,
Agent for Exchange of Prisoners.

HEADQUARTERS DEPARTMENT OF VIRGINIA, 7TH ARMY CORPS,
Fort Monroe, Virginia, January 18, 1863.

SIR: Will you please send me by Captain Mulford a reply to my communication to you of the 14th instant, in reference to your retention of United States officers in violation of the cartel, and also to the case of Mrs. Piggott. Will you also inform me whether you will release the citizen prisoners now held by you, and especially those captured by General Stuart in his raid into Maryland and Pennsylvania.

William J. Peters, whose release you promised me some time ago, has reported to me, with a copy of parole to procure the release of one White, a citizen, or return in thirty days. I should have been glad if his release had been unconditional, as agreed on, but having given his parole, he has diligently, but unsuccessfully, sought out White. Only three Whites have been found on the rolls, two at Fort McHerry and one at Fort Monroe, but all were released some time since. It being impossible to furnish the equivalent named, will you accept for him one Henry Voghler, now held at Baltimore. If so, please notify me through Captain Mulford.

I am, very respectfully, your obedient servant,
WILLIAM H. LUDLOW,
Lieutenant Colonel and Agent for Exchange of Prisoners.
Hon. ROBERT OULD,
Agent for Exchange of Prisoners.

HEADQUARTERS DEPARTMENT OF VIRGINIA, 7TH ARMY CORPS,
Fort Monroe, January 21, 1863.

GENERAL: I have the honor to enclose to you communications just received from Mr. Robert Ould, confederate agent for exchange of prisoners; also a copy of communication of December 11. These show the condition of matters as connected with citizen prisoners. I would recommend that no civilians be released from any of our prisons to go south, unless to procure exchanges. Such exchanges can be made. Before resorting to reprisals, would it not be better to use up all the material for exchanges now on hand? The mail is just closing, and I am obliged to write in haste.

I am, very respectfully, your obedient servant,
WILLIAM H. LUDLOW,
Lieutenant Colonel and Agent for Exchange of Prisoners.
Major General HITCHCOCK,
Commissioner for Exchange of Prisoners.

HEADQUARTERS DEPARTMENT OF VIRGINIA, 7TH ARMY CORPS,
Fort Monroe, January 23, 1863.

Permit me to call your attention to a point in our exchanges, which is operating (though probably unnoticed by you) with great unfairness.

At our last interview, and not anticipating such decisions as you have arrived at in reference to exchanges of United States officers, in order to facilitate our business, I assented to the plan of exchanging by captures, and reducing to equivalents in privates. The result now is, that while I reduced to such equivalent all your officers captured at Fredericksburg, who had been paroled and sent through the lines, you retain all of our officers captured at the same place. Whatever action may be taken in violation of the cartel, in reference to officers captured at Fredericksburg, shall be released on their parole. Will you please send me your decision on this point. The declaration of exchange of our officers and men paroled at Goldsborough, N. C., May 22, 1862, and delivered at Washington, N. C., was only intended to apply to seven, (7,) and not to the large capture referred to by you.

I am, very respectfully, your obedient servant,
WILLIAM H. LUDLOW,
Lieutenant Colonel and Agent for Exchange of Prisoners.
Hon. ROBERT OULD.

CITY POINT, *March* 31, 1863.

SIR: In the delivery of officers which you intend to make to us, you must take into consideration the large number (more than two hundred) whom we have captured, paroled, and released since the President's proclamation. I am entitled to equivalent for them. You can bring in any paroles of a like kind yourself.

Upon your application I recognized this principle in the case of the Fredericksburg officers. Even after I had ceased delivering officers, I surrendered to you of those in our possession a number equal to those whom you paroled at Fredericksburg.

I ask the recognition of the same principle now.

Respectfully, your obedient servant,

ROBERT OULD,
Agent of Exchange.

Lieut. Colonel LUDLOW,
Agent of Exchange.

HEADQUARTERS DEPARTMENT OF VIRGINIA, 7TH ARMY CORPS,
Fort Monroe, Virginia, April 3, 1863.

SIR: I send you to-day ———— prisoners of war. Among them are nine officers, two of whom, Lieutenant A. A. Scott, 6th Alabama volunteers, captured at South Mountain, September 14, 1862, and Captain C. R. Sherman, captured at Georgetown, October 18, 1862, are exchanged.

For the others, Major C. Breckenridge, 2d Virginia cavalry; Major Rufus Wharton, North Carolina sharpshooters; Captain John Alexander, 2d Virginia cavalry; Lieutenant H. B. Bickester, 8th Virginia cavalry; Lieutenant O. H. Cox, 21st Mississippi volunteers; Adjutant T. B. Hutchinson, 8th Virginia cavalry; Lieutenant Charles E. Robinson, 9th Virginia cavalry, I ask equivalents from the Murfreesboro' officers; Captain Mulford is instructed to bring them. Please send me Major D. J. Hall, 89th Illinois, who is one of them. Please send me by Captain Mulford lists of our officers held by you, that I may be enabled to arrange for the delivery of the equivalents in your officers. I desire to know when all our officers, naval and military, will be at Richmond ready for delivery. The revocation of the offensive order of Mr. Jefferson Davis, relating to United States officers and the observance of the cartel, will settle all questions relating to officers. Until this be done, all exchange of officers must be special. I will deliver to you in exchange for United States officers equivalents in number or rank of confederate officers. If we have not the equivalent number in rank, enough of lower grade will be exchanged to secure the release of all you hold. The number of officers captured and paroled by us at Fredericksburg was in excess of United States officers captured at the same place, and delivered by you at City Point. Sergeant Muller, a prisoner of war, has not yet been delivered. Will you send him by this boat? The Murfreesboro' and Arkansas Post prisoners are now on their way here, and are expected to arrive at the rate of 500 daily. Some have already been sent to you.

I am, very respectfully, your obedient servant,

WILLIAM H. LUDLOW,
Lieutenant Colonel and Agent for Exchange of Prisoners.

Hon. ROBERT OULD,
Agent for Exchange of Prisoners.

HEADQUARTERS DEPARTMENT OF VIRGINIA, 7TH ARMY CORPS,
Fort Monroe, April 8, 1863.

SIR: The best mode of arranging all questions relating to exchange of officers is to revoke, formally or informally, the offensive proclamation relating to our officers. I simply ask that you say by authority that such proclamation is revoked. The spirit of that proclamation was the infliction of personal indignities upon our officers, and as long as it remains unrepealed it can be at any moment put in force by your authorities. What assurance have we that it will not be?

I earnestly desire a return to the cartel in all matters pertaining to officers, and until such be the case, and a uniformity of rule be thereby established, our exchange of officers must be special. Some of our officers paroled at Vicksburg, were subsequently placed in close confinement, and are now so held. If hereafter we parole any of your officers, such paroles will be offset against any which you may possess. At present the exchanges will be confined to such equivalents as are held in confinement on either side. I hope you will soon be able to remove all difficulties about officers, by the revocation I have mentioned. By reference to the map, you will see that Fort Delaware is en route to Fort Monroe. It is used as a depot for collecting of prisoners sent from other places for shipment here, and is from its peculiar position well adapted for convenience for exchange.

If any mistake be found in the account of men paroled by Lieutenant Colonel Richards, at Oxford, Mississippi, on December 22, 1862, it can be rectified when we meet.

I am, very respectfully, your obedient servant,
WILLIAM H. LUDLOW,
Lieutenant Colonel and Agent for Exchange of Prisoners.
Hon. ROBERT OULD,
Agent for Exchange of Prisoners.

RICHMOND, *April* 11, 1863.

SIR: Your letters of the 8th instant have been received. I am very much surprised at your refusal to deliver officers for those of your own who have been captured, paroled, and released by us since the date of the proclamation and message of President Davis. That refusal is not only a flagrant breach of the cartel, but can be supported by no rule of reciprocity or equity.

It is utterly useless to argue any such matter.

I assure you that not one officer of any grade will be delivered to you until you change your purpose in that respect.

You have charged us with breaking the cartel. With what sort of justice can that allegation be supported, when you delivered only a few days ago over ninety officers, most of whom had been forced to languish and suffer in prison for months before we were compelled, by that and other reasons, to issue the retaliatory order of which you complain? Those ninety-odd are not one-half of those whom you unjustly hold in prison. On the other hand, I defy you to name the case of one who is confined by us whom our government has declared exchanged.

Is it your idea that we are to be bound by every strictness of the cartel, while you are at liberty to violate it for months, and that, too, not only in a few instances, but in hundreds? You know that our refusal to parole officers was a matter exclusively of retaliation. It was based only upon your refusal to observe the requirements of the cartel. All that you had to do to remove the obnoxious measure of retaliation was to observe the provisions of the cartel, and redress the wrongs which had been perpetrated.

Your last resolution, if persisted in, settles the matter. You need not send any officers to City Point, with the expectation of getting an equivalent in officers, so long as you refuse to deliver any for those whom we have released on parole in Tennessee and Kentucky.

If captivity, privation, and misery are to be the fate of officers on both sides hereafter, let God judge between us. I have struggled in this matter as if it had been a matter of life and death to me. I am heart-sick at the termination, but I have no self reproaches.

Respectfully, your obedient servant,

ROBERT OULD,
Agent of Exchange.

Lieut. Col. WM. H. LUDLOW,
Agent of Exchange.

HEADQUARTERS DEPARTMENT OF VIRGINIA, 7TH ARMY CORPS,
Fort Monroe, April 13, 1863.

SIR: I have just received your letter of the 11th instant, and am too much hurried to reply, as I wish in detail, to the several points therein contained. You are all wrong in your premises, arguments, and conclusions. I agree with you that it is useless to argue the question, and I unite with you in the expression of your earnest desire to alleviate the miseries of captivity of officers who have been so needlessly and so cruelly subjected to it by the proclamation and message of Mr. Jefferson Davis. I will acknowledge all proper paroles of our officers by delivering to you equivalents of our officers, after the special exchanges of those now in confinement are carried out. This is, I believe, what you ask for. Will you frankly inform me if it be the intention of your authorities to put in force the offensive portion of the proclamation and message so often alluded to, when the fortunes of war may place the greater number of our officers in your hands. Your officers are now in Fort Delaware ready for delivery, and your reply will determine whether they are to come for exchange, or to be returned to the west.

Please be clear, frank, and explicit in your reply. Captain Mulford is instructed to bring it to me.

I am, very respectfully, your obedient servant,

WM. H. LUDLOW,
Lieutenant Colonel and Agent for Exchange of Prisoners.

Hon. ROBERT OULD,
Agent for Exchange of Prisoners.

HEADQUARTERS DEPARTMENT OF VIRGINIA, 7TH ARMY CORPS,
Fort Monroe, April 20, 1863.

SIR: On the 11th instant I sent to City Point, in charge of Lieutenant Colonel Matson, ten (10) confederate officers who had not been exchanged. I enclose herewith a copy of my letter of that date, giving the names and rank of the officers. Lieutenant Colonel Matson disobeyed his instructions in not bringing back with him equivalents for these officers. Please deliver these equivalents now to the officer bearing this.

In my letter of the 13th instant, a copy of which is enclosed for your more convenient reference, I stated my willingness to exchange officers on the terms therein mentioned. I wish to know whether those terms are assented to by you and I desire a response to the other questions therein propounded. The peculiar position of this question of exchange of officers renders these questions proper, and I regret extremely having received, through my agent, so unsatisfactory, and I may say exceptionable notice, (not reply,) of which I enclose a copy. Until you think proper to inform me what your understanding is in reference to our officers, I certainly cannot move one step further toward sending to City Point any of the large number of confederate officers, now at Fort Delaware, awaiting your action.

I again ask the release of Lieutenant Colonel Douglass Hapeman and Major J. H. Widmer, 104th regiment Illinois volunteers. Hartsville officers declared exchanged, and yet held by you. Please send them, and also one (1) captain and one (1) lieutenant due to me, as you will see on reference to my letter of the 13th instant, and which enclosed duplicate lists of officers sent to you.

I am, very respectfully, your obedient servant.

WM. H. LUDLOW,
Lieutenant Colonel and Agent for Exchange of Prisoners.

Hon. ROBERT OULD,
Agent for Exchange of Prisoners.

RICHMOND, *April* 22, 1863.

SIR: Your communication of the 21st has been received. I did not answer your communication of the 13th instant, because I really had nothing more to say in relation to the subject-matter than what was contained in the letter to which that was a reply. In my unofficial note to Captain Mulford, I certainly did not intend to be discourteous, or to write anything "exceptionable." You will do me the justice to acknowledge that in all the difficult and irritating subjects which have engaged our attention in correspondence, I have never stepped beyond the bounds of decorous propriety. I take pleasure in saying the same in reference to yourself.

In my former communications, and in personal interview, I demanded that equivalents should be given for the officers whom we had paroled and released, since the 10th of December last, in Tennessee and Kentucky. I distinctly put those officers upon the same footing as that of those whom we now hold in confinement I only asked that in exchange, officers paroled and released should be put in the same category as those who were retained.

You had complained that we did not parole your officers. Although, in your communication of the 13th, you agreed to give equivalents for such officers as we had retained, you refused to give any at present for those whom we had paroled and released. In other words, in cases where we had pursued a course which you had declared objectionable, an equivalent would be given; but where we had conformed to your own demands in the release of officers, none should be given. I must confess I was very much surprised at your letter of the 8th instant. I expressed that surprise in perhaps very strong language in my communication of the 11th instant. I intended in that letter to say to you very distinctly, that unless the released officers in the west were put upon the same footing as those whom we held in confinement, no more deliveries of officers would be made to you. I came to the determination with great regret. Your letter of the 13th did not mend matters much. I thought our demand was so fair, so equitable, that no one could refuse it. When, therefore, you sought, in your communication of the 13th, to put the released western officers upon a different footing from those held by us, I considered that you refused to acknowledge our fair claim.

In your letter of the 13th instant you say, "I will acknowledge all proper paroles of our officers, by delivering to you equivalents of your officers, after the special exchanges of those now in confinement are carried out." That was not what I asked. I demanded simply that the western released officers should be put upon the same footing with those held by us. I did not wish to have any controversy about "proper paroles," nor did I think it right that such cases should be postponed until all those in our custody were released. I thought, and still think, that the exchange should be simultaneous. You have an excess of officers—more, perhaps, than those now held by us, added to such as we have paroled.

One boat can accommodate all. Why, then, postpone the delivery of equivalents, except to allow distracting questions to intervene, which might defeat the delivery? If you have any paroles, I will acknowledge them; if any are hereafter presented by you, up to the present date, I will acknowledge *them*, if you will give me the same privilege. What can be more fair, equal, and reciprocal than all this? If you think I will press upon you paroles which are not "proper," let us meet together when the officers are brought up, or before. I will offer none to you but such as are most clearly within our former rules of practice. If you will send to City Point all the officers you have, you will receive no detriment.

If there are more than we have, (counting paroles,) I pledge you an equivalent, either in men already delivered to you, or, if you prefer it, in officers hereafter captured, and as soon as captured.

No proclamation or message shall affect the surplus.

Respectfully, your obedient servant,
ROBERT OULD,
Agent of Exchange.

Lieut. Colonel WM. H. LUDLOW,
Agent of Exchange.

HEADQUARTERS DEPARTMENT OF VIRGINIA, 7TH ARMY CORPS,
Fort Monroe, May 22, 1863.

SIR: I have the honor to enclose to you copies of General Orders No. 49 and No. 100 of War Department, announcing regulations and instructions for the government of the United States forces in the field, in the matter of paroles. These, together with the stipulations of the cartel, will govern our army. I would invite your special attention to article 7 of the cartel, which provides that all prisoners of war shall be sent to places of delivery therein specified. The execution of this article will obviate much discussion and difficulty, growing out of the mode, time, and place of giving paroles. No paroles or exchanges will be considered binding, except those, under the stipulations of said article, permitting commanders of two opposing armies to exchange or release on parole at other points mutually agreed on by said commanders.

I am, very respectfully, your obedient servant,
WM. H. LUDLOW,
Lieutenant Colonel and Agent for Exchange of Prisoners.

Hon. ROBERT OULD,
Agent for Exchange of Prisoners.

EXCHANGE OF PRISONERS.   11

CONFEDERATE STATES OF AMERICA,
War Department, Richmond, Virginia, May 22, 186 .

SIR: In several of your late communications you have appealed to me for the release of political prisoners held by us. I am ready to deliver every one of them when you do the same charity. Until then not one of them shall be released, except at our own pleasure. You asked, in a late communication, for the release of the sheriff of Barbour county. Are you aware that you now hold some half dozen or more of harmless and inoffensive old men as hostages, whom you do not even pretend to release, and yet ask the sheriff's deliverance? You have now thousands of helpless non-combatants in your prisons—not arrested as dangerous persons to your armies, but incarcerated because it is supposed they are loyal to their own country. Their number is increasing every day. I will listen to no proposition for the release of non-combatants that is not based upon the delivery of all whom you have in custody, coupled with some distinct written understanding as to future conduct in respect to such captures.

If this is not agreeable, let God save the right. I hope there will be no further mistake between us in regard to this matter. I trust I have made myself sufficiently distinct.

Respectfully, your obedient servant,

ROBERT OULD,
Agent of Exchange.

Lieut. Colonel WM. H. LUDLOW,
Agent of Exchange.

CONFEDERATE STATES OF AMERICA,
War Department, Richmond, Virginia, May 22, 1863.

SIR: You are very well aware that for the last six months I have been presenting to you lists of confederate officers and soldiers and confederate citizens who have been detained by your authorities in their prisons. Some of them, upon my remonstrance, have been released and sent to us. By far the greater number still remain in captivity. I am satisfied that you have made strenuous exertions to have those persons released, and to carry out in good faith the agreements which we have made. Even those exertions have proved of little avail.

Nothing now remains but for me to give you formal notice that our government will resort to retaliation in every case which has heretofore been brought to your attention where the wrong complained of has not been redressed. The confederate authorities will exercise their discretion in selecting such prisoners as they think best, whether officers or privates, in this purpose of retaliation. You will be notified in each case. I am now preparing a list of such officers and men as are reserved for retaliation. As soon as the parties for whom they are held are delivered to us, the hostages will be released.

I have thus frankly informed you of our purposes before they are put into actual execution, for the double purpose of preventing any imputation of bad faith and of giving you an opportunity of saving a resort to so stern a remedy. You have at this moment, in your prisons, confederate officers whom you have held over twelve months without charges or trial. They have been fairly exchanged by our agreements, and ought to have been delivered long ago.

Respectfully, your obedient servant,

ROBERT OULD,
Agent of Exchange.

Lieut. Colonel WM. H. LUDLOW.

HEADQUARTERS DEPARTMENT OF VIRGINIA,
Seventh Army Corps, Fort Monroe, May 25, 1563.

SIR: You threaten retaliation in your letter of the 22d instant, in case certain parties whom you have demanded are not delivered to you. I beg leave to inform you that no deliveries of any kind will be made to you under such threats. If such threats are withdrawn, deliveries can be made of parties properly entitled to release, but not otherwise. Three-fourths or nine-tenths of the cases of which you have furnished memoranda have been released and delivered to you. If, before the necessary investigations in the remaining cases have been made, you put in practice retaliation, either upon our officers or men, I give you formal notice that the United States government will exercise their discretion in selecting such persons as they think best, whether officers or privates, for the purpose of counter retaliation.

I am, very respectfully, your obedient servant,
WM. H. LUDLOW,
Lieutenant Colonel and Agent for Exchange of Prisoners.

Hon. ROBERT OULD,
Agent for Exchange of Prisoners.

CITY POINT, *May* 31, 1863.

SIR: I call your attention again to a matter of which I often heretofore complained. By to-day's arrival you have sent several citizens as prisoners of war, and several discharged soldiers, as also prisoners of war.

One of the men, T. H. Moreland, is put down as belonging to the 1st Kentucky cavalry, who never was in our service in any sort of capacity in his life; who never was in the field, and not even a guerilla or bushwhacker. Captain Mulford heard his statement. He says he was compelled to sign a parole at Louisville as a member of the 1st Kentucky cavalry, under a threat if he did not so do he would be put in prison with ball and chain during the war. He protested against it in the hearing of more than fifty men here, who were here this very day. There are four or five other cases of exactly the same sort in your roll delivered to me this day.

The memoranda are made on your roll. Is this to be allowed?

Respectfully, your obedient servant,
ROBERT OULD,
Agent of Exchange.

Lieut. Colonel WILLIAM H. LUDLOW,
Agent of Exchange.

CITY POINT, *June* 1, 1863.

SIR: I was about proceeding to Fortress Monroe, or as near to it as I would be allowed to go, when Captain Mulford came up the river. I am afraid your proceeding in relation to declarations of the exchanges of your men will lead to complication and difficulty. The Holly Springs capture, according to my recollection, pays off the number due to you at our last interview. You have not sent more than six hundred since, including to-day's arrival. For that number you declare exchanged five regiments, (91st Illinois, 51st Indiana, 73d Indiana, 3d Ohio, and 80th Illinois,) also the captures at Mount Sterling, and the men of the Indianola.

How many the Mount Sterling capture are I do not know, but I am very sure the aggregate of the above greatly exceeds the balance due to you.

I protest against the declarations of exchange where the number is not known and agreed upon by us. You can readily perceive without my statement what grave objections might be made to such a proceeding. Why not make exchanges by rolls of which we can have a copy, and in relation to which we have mutually agreed, as in the Holly Spring capture? How am I to know how many men of the 80th Illinois regiment were taken prisoners, or when or where they were captured? I throw out these observations as suggestions for your reflection. I think you will agree with me that when we or you are in excess of prisoners, neither party should declare any exchange except where the lists have been adjusted between us, and the number declared to be exchanged known and agreed on between us. I do not so much object to your overrunning the number due to you, as the certainty of great complication and prospect of misunderstanding by pursuing the course you have done in this case.

You have not given me any reply even yet to my inquiries in relation to your declaration of exchange as to parties captured at Muldeaughi hill, or the 66th Indiana. I hope I shall not be compelled to wait much longer.

Respectfully, your obedient servant,
ROBERT OULD,
Agent of Exchange.

Lieut. Colonel WILLIAM H. LUDLOW,
Agent of Exchange.

HEADQUARTERS DEPARTMENT OF VIRGINIA, 7TH ARMY CORPS,
Fort Monroe, June 3, 1863.

SIR: You informed me at our last interview that you were instructed not to deliver any of the officers of Colonel Straight's command captured at or near Cedar Bluff, Georgia, about the first of May last. I now make a formal demand for them under the cartel, and tender to you their equivalents in your own officers now in our hands. If this demand and tender be refused, please frankly state the reasons therefor, that the issues presented may be fully understood and promptly met.

I am, very respectfully, your obedient servant,
WILLIAM H. LUDLOW,
Lieutenant Colonel and Agent for Exchange of Prisoners.
Hon. ROBERT OULD,
Agent for Exchange of Prisoners.

HEADQUARTERS DEPARTMENT OF VIRGINIA, 7TH ARMY CORPS,
Fort Monroe, Virginia, June 3, 1863.

SIR: Will you please furnish me with a copy of the act of the confederate congress, which you promised me, and which directs some certain disposition of our captured officers commanding negro troops, and also of the troops themselves.

Will you also please inform me if it be the intention of your authorities to execute this act.

I am, very respectfully, your obedient servant,
WILLIAM H. LUDLOW,
Lieutenant Colonel and Agent for Exchange of Prisoners.
Hon. ROBERT OULD,
Agent for Exchange of Prisoners.

CONFEDERATE STATES OF AMERICA,
War Department, Richmond, Virginia, June 5, 1863.

SIR: You ask me for a frank statement of the reason for the detention of the officers of Straight's command. I will give it to you, as I will in every case when you ask it. I think you will find it franker than your answer to any inquiry as to whether you intended to deliver the officers who have heretofore been declared exchanged.

Allegations have been officially received from the highest authority in Alabama, charging these officers with grave offences, as well against the laws of that State as the usages of civilized warfare. They are detained until the proper inquiry can be made and the fact ascertained, when a determination will be made by the confederate government, whether they come within the obligations of the cartel as prisoners of war, or are to be dealt with as criminals against the laws of war and the State. These men have never been declared exchanged. I believe I have given you a better and certainly a more detailed reason for their detention than you did with reference to Colonel Morehead and other exchanged officers of whom I inquired, and about whom all I could learn was that they were confined in Fort Norfolk, under recent orders from the Secretary of War.

Respectfully, your obedient servant,
ROBERT OULD,
Agent of Exchange.

Lieut. Colonel WILLIAM H. LUDLOW,
Agent of Exchange.

CONFEDERATE STATES OF AMERICA,
War Department, Richmond, Virginia, June 5, 1863.

SIR: I again ask you, will you deliver the officers and men whom our agreements have declared exchanged? Will you not give me an answer to this inquiry? Allow me to quote you, "I now make a formal demand for them under the cartel. If this demand be refused, please frankly state the reason therefor, that issues presented may be fully understood and promptly met."

You say I am mistaken in stating that no federal officers are in our prisons who have been declared exchanged. You promise to furnish memoranda.

You actually refer to one case, that of one Spencer Kellog. I have no recollection of ever having heard of him before. I have already caused inquiry to be made, and if he is here he shall be delivered to you. So shall each and every other officer or man who has been declared exchanged, if you will say you will do the same. I do not care whether there are charges against them or not. If you wish to limit this to officers, I will agree to it. I would prefer it should include the men. Prepare your lists. I have prepared mine. Bring even the men whose deliverance I have asked, and who are already exchanged, and you shall have, at City Point, every prisoner whom you can name as being confined in our territory. If any one is wanting I will pay you tenfold. Will you agree to this? I have told you often, and repeat it now, that there is no reciprocal and fair proposition as to prisoners and exchanges to which I will not agree.

I again say that it is my deliberate conviction that there is not one solitary exchanged federal officer now in confinement in the south, unless Dr. Rucker is made an exception. I honestly believe that you have now in your prisons, or on parole confined to the north, more than two hundred exchanged confederate officers. You must allow me to say that I was amused at the list which you returned me some time ago; I refer to that which purported to be an answer to the specific cases I had brought to your attention. More than one-half of the cases had "no record" appended to them. Such an entry was made in reference to Dr. Greene; the same as to Clagett Fitzhugh, to Parson Clameron, to Kerchival, and to a hundred others, who have been seen by scores of people within a month or two. Every man on that list, except such as you have already delivered, is now in some one of your prisons. He may not be in the one named; if not, it is because he has been removed in accordance with the tactics of your government or its jailers. I ask again, will you deliver our exchanged officers and men?

Respectfully, your obedient servant,

R. OULD,
Agent of Exchange.

Lieut. Colonel WILLIAM H. LUDLOW,
Agent of Exchange.

CONFEDERATE STATES OF AMERICA,
War Department, Richmond, Virginia, June 5, 1863.

SIR: Will you be good enough to inform me when it is to be considered that General Order No. 100 went into effect. Is the date of the order April 24, 1863, or the date of its communication to me, 23d May, 1863, the true time? Do you recognize the rules of General Order No. 100 to be as binding against you as for you?

Permit me also to call your attention to the flagrant outrages that have recently been perpetrated in Gloucester, Matthews, King and Queen, and the adjacent counties. Are they a fair interpretation of your celebrated general order? I am aware it gives a license for a man to be either a friend or a gentleman. He can find abundant authority for either role in the order. What is the interpretation in General Dix's department? The country has always esteemed him as an honorable gentleman. I enclose a slip, which is inside the truth, recounting some of the doings of Colonel Kilpatrick. Does General Dix approve of this style of conducting war, even with belligerent rebels? It is in his own department. Perhaps the higher powers may have something to do with this question some of these days. "Silent spectators of the destruction of their agricultural implements."

Respectfully, your obedient servant,

R. OULD,
Agent of Exchange.

Lieut. Colonel WILLIAM H. LUDLOW,
Agent of Exchange.

CONFEDERATE STATES OF AMERICA,
War Department, Richmond, Virginia, June 12, 1863.

SIR: I enclose to you the resolution of congress in relation to retaliation. I thought you had seen it in the papers transmitted to you, otherwise I would have sent it. I take it for granted that the confederate authorities purpose to carry out a resolution solemnly passed by them. I have not asked them whether they intend to do so, and I do not think I will ever be so inconsiderate as to make any such inquiry. I have thus frankly given my view as to this matter; and I beg leave to ask you in return whether it is the purpose of your government to execute its conscription act; and further, how many men will be raised under its provisions. I feel so deep a personal interest in that subject, that I hope I have not transgressed any propriety in propounding the inquiry, after the example you have set me.

Respectfully, your obedient servant,

R. OULD,
Agent of Exchange.

Lieut. Colonel WILLIAM H. LUDLOW,
Agent of Exchange.

CONFEDERATE STATES OF AMERICA,
War Department, Richmond, Virginia, June 12, 1863.

SIR: You are mistaken in supposing that my "proposition to have the releases from paroles and oaths cover other than parties delivered at City Point" was made after I had published notice No. 5. It was made before that date, (May 11th,) and after a full and deliberate discussion between us. You hesitated at first; but when I assured you it only extended to cases of parties who were allowed to leave your territory and come to us, whether by City Point or otherwise, you assented to it in distinct and unequivocal terms. The same provision, in principle, was incorporated in exchange notice No. 4, January 13, 1863. You recognized the same principle in numerous exchanges made after that date, and before May 11, 1863. I have now given the notice in good faith. You can stop its application after May 6th, if you choose to do so. I cannot agree that you shall nullify the notice already given; all persons embraced in it are entirely free from any obligations made by them. It was so distinctly agreed upon between us that there can be no mistake about it. Nothing will make me consent that such men shall be put under any ban or disability, by reason of any action of theirs performed on the faith of this notice. You can have your veto as to the future, but not as to the past. If any penalties are visited upon them, it becomes the solemn duty of the confederate government to throw every protection in its power around them. I am sure it will do so.

Respectfully, your obedient servant,

R. OULD,
Agent of Exchange.

Lieut. Colonel WILLIAM H. LUDLOW,
Agent of Exchange.

HEADQUARTERS DEPARTMENT OF VIRGINIA,
Seventh Army Corps, Fort Monroe, June 14, 1863.

SIR: I assure you that you have not transgressed any propriety in your questions as to the purpose of the United States government to execute its conscription act, and as to the number of men who will be raised under its provisions. I have the honor to inform you, in reply, that the conscription act is now being executed, and that a sufficient number of men will be raised under its provisions to bring this war to a speedy and successful conclusion.

My object in requesting from you a copy of the act of the confederate congress, and information as to intentions to execute it, was to know officially what disposition under the act was proposed to be made of officers and men captured in arms, and who had been duly mustered into the service of the United States, and also that the issues thereby presented could be fully understood and promptly met.

Sections 4, 5, 6 and 7 of this act propose a gross and inexcusable breach of the cartel, both in letter and spirit. Upon reference to the cartel, you will find no mention whatever of what was to be the color of prisoners of war. It was unnecessary to make any such mention, for, before the establishment of this cartel, and before one single negro or mulatto was mustered into the United States service, you had them organized in arms in Louisiana. You had Indians, and half-breed negroes and Indians, organized in arms under Albert Pike, in Arkansas. Subsequently, negroes were captured on the battle-field at Antietam, and delivered as prisoners of war at Aiken's Landing, to the confederate authorities, and receipted for and counted in exchange. And, more recently, the confederate legislature of Tennessee have passed an act forcing into their military service (I quote literally) all male free persons of color, between the ages of fifteen and fifty, or such number as may be necessary, who may be sound in body and capable of actual service; and they further enacted, that in the event a sufficient number of free persons of color to meet the wants of the State shall not tender their services, then the governor is empowered, through the sheriffs of different counties, to impress such persons, until the required number is obtained.

But it is needless to argue the question. You have not a foot of ground to stand upon in making the proposed discrimination among our captured officers and men. I protest against it as a violation of the cartel, of the laws and usages of war, and of your own practices under them.

Passing events will clearly show the impracticability in executing the act referred to. In case, however, the attempt be made to execute it, I now give you formal notice that the United States government will throw its protection around all its officers and men, without regard to color, and will promptly retaliate for all cases violating the cartel, or the laws and usages of war.

I am, very respectfully, your obedient servant,
WILLIAM H. LUDLOW,
Lieutenant Colonel and Agent for Exchange of Prisoners.
Hon. ROBERT OULD,
Agent for Exchange of Prisoners.

HEADQUARTERS DEPARTMENT OF VIRGINIA,
7th Army Corps, Fort Monroe, June 14, 1863.

SIR: General Order No. 100 is considered as having gone into effect from the date of its communication to you, on the 23d of May last, and is, of course, mutually binding.

I am, very respectfully, your obedient servant,
WILLIAM H. LUDLOW,
Lieutenant Colonel and Agent for Exchange of Prisoners.
Hon. ROBERT OULD,
Agent for Exchange of Prisoners.

CONFEDERATE STATES OF AMERICA,
War Department, Richmond, Virginia, June 19, 1863.

SIR: On the 5th day of June, 1863, I requested you to inform me when General Order No. 100 was considered as going into effect. To that you have returned no answer. Its date is April 24, 1863. You delivered it to me on the 23d of May, 1863.

I perceive by a General Order No. 15, March 9, 1863, issued by General

Schenck, that all officers and men who had been captured in his department, and particularly exchanged, should return to duty and service, on penalty of being considered deserters. When you delivered General Order No. 100 to me, I inquired of you as to the date when it went into effect. I understood you to say the date of its delivery. You may, therefore, well imagine my surprise when I perceive that, by the General Order of one of your own departmental commanders, the new provisions as to paroles are not only to have effect from and after March 9, 1863, but are made to apply to all cases previous to that date, without any limitation as to time. This is not only contrary to your own declarations to me, but to our common practice up to May 23, 1863. You have charged against me and received credit for several captures made by General Stoneman's command, in his recent raid. Is it pretended that you are to have credit for captures made by your commands, while none is to be given to us, precisely under the same circumstances? Is this fair, or just, or right?

Respectfully, your obedient servant,

ROBERT OULD,
Agent of Exchange.

Lieut. Colonel WILLIAM H. LUDLOW,
Agent of Exchange.

CONFEDERATE STATES OF AMERICA,
War Department, Richmond, Virginia, July 1, 1863.

SIR: The clear understanding between us as to civilians was that all who had been paroled, or put under any bonds, or who had taken any oath of allegiance, were released from condition of parole, bond and oath, where such civilians were delivered to their own people. It was confined to such as were released and delivered. Such is the fair and proper interpretation of paragraph 8 of notice 5. It would, perhaps, have been better for me to have added the word "delivered" after "released." I did not do so because persons who were *sent* into our lines might not consider themselves as being delivered. I have, however, assured all persons that it only embraces such persons as were delivered to me or my agents, or such as were sent into our lines. If you continue to take exception to the phraseology, I will correct it in my next notice.

Respectfully, your obedient servant,

ROBERT OULD,
Agent of Exchange.

Lieut. Colonel WILLIAM H. LUDLOW,
Agent of Exchange.

HEADQUARTERS DEPARTMENT OF VIRGINIA,
7th Army Corps, Fort Monroe, July 7, 1863.

SIR: I herewith enclose to you a copy of General Order No. 207, which contains some additional provisions to those mentioned in my communication to you of the 22d May last. It is understood that officers of the United States and confederate officers have, at various times and places, paroled and released prisoners of war, not in accordance with the cartel.

The government of the United States will not recognize and will not expect the confederate authorities to recognize such unauthorized paroles. Prisoners released on parole not authorized by the cartel, after my notice to you of the 22d of May, will not be regarded as prisoners of war and will not be exchanged.

When prisoners of war have been released, without the delivery specified in the cartel, since the 22d May last, such release will be regarded as unconditional, and the prisoners released as subject to orders without exchange, the same as if they had never been captured.

I am, very respectfully, your obedient servant,
WILLIAM H. LUDLOW,
Lieutenant Colonel and Agent for Exchange of Prisoners.

Hon. ROBERT OULD,
Agent for Exchange of Prisoners.

HEADQUARTERS DEPARTMENT OF VIRGINIA,
7th Army Corps, Fort Monroe, July 14, 1863.

SIR: I decline to unite with you in your declaration of the exchange of the officers named by you in your communication of the 13th instant just received, and who form a part of those captured at Vicksburg.

In violation of the cartel you now hold in close confinement many of our officers, though their release was long ago demanded and their equivalents tendered to you. You even permitted these equivalents to be sent back to Fort Monroe, from City Point. In this position of affairs, and being in entire ignorance of what you propose to do with our officers now in your hands, I must decline any special arrangements until we meet. This meeting, with your consent, will take place as soon as I shall have received the paroles of the Vicksburg captures. Please, therefore, notify the officers named by you, that their exchange cannot be recognized by our authorities until the declarations be united in by me.

In making arrangements with you for exchanges of paroles of officers, I shall expect to exhaust equivalents of equal rank before we take up those of higher rank.

To settle all difficulties connected with exchanges of officers, I again invite you to a return to the cartel; and if you refuse, I again ask you, why such refusal?

I am, very respecfully, your obedient servant,
WILLIAM H. LUDLOW,
Lieutenant Colonel and Agent for Exchange of Prisoners.

Hon. ROBERT OULD,
Agent for Exchange of Prisoners.

P. S.—The declaration of exchange made by you on the 2d instant leaves you in debt to me between eight and nine hundred men.

HEADQUARTERS DEPARTMENT OF VIRGINIA,
7th Army Corps, Fort Monroe, July 15, 1863.

SIR: In the letter of July 8, of the Hon. Alexander H. Stephens to Hon. Jefferson Davis, giving a report of his mission, appears the following statement: The reasons assigned for the refusal by the United States Secretary of War, to wit, that "the customary agents and channels are considered adequate for all needful military communications and conferences," to one acquainted with the facts, seem not only unsatisfactory, but very singular and unaccountable; for it is certainly known to him that these very agents, to whom he evidently alludes, heretofore agreed upon in a formal conference in reference to the exchange of prisoners, (one of the subjects embraced in your letter to me,) are now, and have been for some time, distinctly at issue on several important points.

The existing cartel, owing to these disagreements, is virtually suspended so far as the exchange of officers on either side is concerned.

As in this statement Mr. Stephens appears to be unacquainted with the facts, may I ask if you will inform him that exchanges of prisoners of war, and the settlement of the intricate and troublesome questions connected therewith, were being proceeded with successfully by us until the issue of the proclamation of the Hon. Jefferson Davis on the 23d of December last, which, in gross violation of the cartel, reserved for execution certain of our captured officers and men. Will you also please inform Mr. Stephens that, in your and my anxious desire to alleviate the horrors of war, the proclamation after a little delay was ignored, and exchanges of officers were resumed. That the exchanges were again interrupted in May last by the operation of an act of the confederate congress, which was another gross violation of the cartel and the laws and usages of war, and which consigned to execution and other punishments certain of our captured officers and men. Will you please furnish Mr. Stephens with a copy of my communication to you and protest of the 14th of June last on this subject, and also inform him that, under that act of the confederate congress, your authorities now retain in close confinement large numbers of our officers, though their release has been demanded and equivalents in your officers tendered, which equivalents have been sent back to Fort Monroe from City Point. Please also inform him that I have again and again invited your authorities to a return to the cartel in exchanges of officers, and that such invitation has not been responded to.

I cannot but believe that, with a statement of these plain facts so well known to you and me, Mr. Stephens will readily see that your authorities are alone at fault, and that he will, in the humane spirit with which he entered on his mission, earnestly recommend the ignoring or repeal of the act of your congress, which is such a clear violation of the cartel, and the fruitful, I may say only source of the practical difficulties now surrounding the exchange of officers.

I have indulged the hope that the magnanimous treatment of your officers captured at Vicksburg and their release upon parole would have prompted the immediate release on parole of all our officers held by you. That hope I have not abandoned.

I am, very respectfully, your obedient servant,
WILLIAM H. LUDLOW,
Lieutenant Colonel and Agent for Exchange of Prisoners.

Hon. ROBERT OULD,
Agent for Exchange of Prisoners.

CONFEDERATE STATES OF AMERICA,
War Department, Richmond, Virginia, July 17, 1863.

SIR: In my communication to you of the 13th instant, declining the exchange of certain officers who had been captured and paroled at Vicksburg, I only did what you yourself have frequently done. On at least one occasion you went further than I presumed to go. You declared your men exchanged, when you had no equivalents to offer. You say, in your letter of the 14th instant, that you decline to unite with me in my declaration, and request me to notify the officers that their exchange cannot be recognized. I call your attention to the 5th article of the cartel, which provides that "each party, upon the discharge of prisoners of the other party, is authorized to discharge an equal number of their own officers or men from parole." I have exercised a clear right under the cartel—one that you have exercised over again and again. I have already delivered to you the equivalents of these officers, which equivalents you may declare exchanged.

My right to declare these officers exchanged does not depend upon your assent.

After I have given you equivalents their exchange is perfected by my declaration, whether you decline to unite with me or not. I shall not, therefore, give the notice which you request.

The officers referred to are already rightfully and properly exchanged. The right to declare officers and men exchanged, where equivalents have been delivered, is one that I cannot yield, and I am unwilling to bind myself by an agreement not to exercise that right "until we meet."

Respectfully, your obedient servant,

ROBERT OULD,
Agent of Exchange.

Lieut. Colonel WM. H. LUDLOW,
Agent of Exchange.

NEW YORK, *July* 22, 1863.

SIR: Your communication of the 15th instant has been forwarded to me here. There is no authority in the cartel for your proposed declaration of exchange of your officers captured at Vicksburg, in the manner you indicate.

The cartel provides for exchange of equal rank until such are exhausted, and then for equivalents. In consequence of the very much larger number of your officers and men we hold on parole and in confinement, you can give no equivalents for the general officers you desire to have exchanged. You cannot for a moment assume that you can select a general officer and declare his equivalents in those of inferior rank, when we hold the paroles of your officers of the same rank as the latter. But even supposing this arrangement was permitted by the cartel, I do not see how you could avail yourself of it at this time.

You will recollect that since the proclamation of the Hon. Jefferson Davis of December last, and more especially since the passage of the act of the confederate congress in reference to our captured officers, both of which were in violation of the cartel, and have caused in the one case a temporary, and in the other a continued suspension of exchanges of officers, all such exchanges have been subjects of special agreement between us.

To avoid the complications and annoyances of these special agreements, I have again and again urged you to a return of the cartel, but up to the present moment in vain. On the contrary, you retain in close confinement large numbers of our officers, for whom I have made a demand and tendered equivalents.

Until you consent to return to the terms prescribed by the cartel for exchange of officers, I shall not consent to any exchanges of them, except on special agreements. I repeat to you that I decline to unite in your proposed declaration of exchange of officers captured at Vicksburg; and if recaptured, they will be dealt with as violators of their paroles. Ought you not, in justice to these officers, to notify them of the exact condition of their cases, and thus enable them to avoid being placed in false positions?

If you are authorized to deliver our officers now held in close confinement, and to a return to the cartel in exchanges of all officers and men, all the complicated questions which have arisen within the last few months can be promptly disposed of.

I am, very respectfully, your obedient servant,

WILLIAM H. LUDLOW,
Lieutenant Colonel and Agent for Exchange of Prisoners.

Hon. ROBERT OULD,
Agent for Exchange of Prisoners.

CONFEDERATE STATES OF AMERICA,
War Department, Richmond, Va., July 26, 1863.

SIR: Your communication of the 22d contests my declaration of exchanges of officers made on the 17th instant. You say "the cartel provides for the exchange of equal ranks until such are exhausted, and then for equivalents." If you had been at Fortress Monroe, where you could have seen the cartel, instead of New York, from which your letter is dated, you would have written no such paragraph. There is nothing in the cartel which contains any such doctrine, or which favors it. Every provision is against it. Your own and my practice has been opposed to it. I again say to you what I have already stated in my communication of the 17th instant, that your assent is not needed to the declared exchange, and I shall not notify the officers whom I have declared exchanged, as you request. I have allowed you to declare exchanges when the number of prisoners in our hands has been the greater. This has been the case from the day when we first met, in the fall of last year, to the capture at Vicksburg. Now, when you have scarcely received official advices of your superiority in prisoners, you boast of the fact, and declare that I cannot give an equivalent for the general officers I have declared exchanged. The point you make is worth nothing, even as you have stated it. You know we have no lieutenant generals or major generals of yours in our hands. For that reason I have declared them exchanged in privates or inferior officers, at your election. I had the right, under the cartel, to make the choice myself; but I preferred that you should do it, and, therefore, I gave you the notification which I did. If, at any time, you present officers for exchange who have been paroled, and we have no officers of similar rank on parole, you can declare their exchanges in privates. If, at this time, you have any officers of the rank I have declared exchanged, or of any other rank, or if you have any particular organization of privates or non-commissioned officers whom you wish exchanged, you have only to state such fact and your selection will be approved. If you hold the paroles of our officers of any rank, as you state, you have only to present them, and whatever is in our hands, whether on parole or in captivity, will be freely given in exchange for them. You say you have again and again invited me to a return to the cartel. Now that our official connexion is being terminated, I say to you in the fear of God, and I appeal to Him for the truth of the declaration, that there has been no single moment, from the time when we were first brought together in connexion with the matter of exchange to the present hour, during which there has not been an open and notorious violation of the cartel by your authorities. Officers and men, numbering over hundreds, have been, during your whole connexion with the cartel, kept in cruel confinement, sometimes in irons or doomed cells, without charges or trial. They are in prison now, without God in His mercy has released them. In our parting moments, let me do you the justice to say that I do not believe it is so much your fault as that of your authorities. Nay more; I believe your removal from your position has been owing to the personal efforts you have made for a faithful observance, not only of the cartel, but of humanity in the conduct of the war.

Again and again have I importuned you to tell me of one officer or man now held in confinement by us who was declared exchanged. You have to these appeals furnished one, Spencer Kellog. For him I have searched in vain. On the other hand, I appeal to your own records for the cases where your reports have shown that our officers and men have been held for long months, and even years, in violation of the cartel and our agreements. The last phase of the enormity, however, exceeds all others. Although you have many thousands of our soldiers now in confinement in your prisons, and especially in that horrible hold of death, Fort Delaware, you have not for several weeks sent us any prisoners. During those weeks you have despatched Captain Mulford with the steamer New York, to City Point three or four times without any prisoners. For the first two or three times some sort of an excuse was attempted. None is given at this present arrival. I do not mean to be offensive when I say that effrontery could not give one. I ask you with no purpose of disrespect, what can you think of this covert attempt to secure the delivery of all your prisoners in our hands, without the release of those of ours, who were languishing in hopeless misery in your prisons and dungeons?

Respectfully, your obedient servant,

ROBERT OULD,
Agent of Exchange.

Colonel W. H. LUDLOW,
Agent of Exchange.

CONFEDERATE STATES OF AMERICA,
War Department, Richmond, Virginia, August 1, 1863.

SIR: In the "Army and Navy Official Gazette," of the date of July 14, 1863, I find a letter of Lieutenant Colonel William H. Ludlow, of the date of July 7, 1863, addressed to Colonel J. C. Kelton. In it is the following paragraph, to wit:

"I have the honor also to state that since the 22d of May last, it has been distinctly understood between Mr. Ould and myself that all captures must be reduced to possession, and that all paroles are to be disregarded, unless taken under the special arrangement of commanding officers of armies in the field, as prescribed in section 7 of the cartel."

If Lieutenant Colonel Ludlow means that he had declared to me that such was the rule which had been adopted by the United States in relation to captures and paroles, to go into effect from and after May 23, 1863, he is entirely right. If he means that I at any time consented to adopt or acquiesce in any such rule, he is entirely wrong. All that passed between us on that subject is in writing. The correspondence will interpret itself.

Respectfully, your obedient servant,

ROBERT OULD,
Agent of Exchange.

Brigadier General S. A. MEREDITH,
Agent of Exchange.

OFFICE OF COMMISSION FOR EXCHANGE,
Fort Monroe, Virginia, August 7, 1863.

GENERAL: I have the honor to inform you that by to-day's boat I have received a most earnest and pressing request from Mr. Ould to grant him a meeting as early as possible. I have not yet sought an interview with him, for the reason that Colonel Ludlow has been quite reticent in regard to matters connected with his late business, nor did I wish to see Mr. Ould until I had some specific instructions from the War Department.

From what I can gather in Colonel Ludlow's letter-books, I suppose the following are points to be insisted upon:

1st. The immediate exchange of Colonel Streight and his command.

2d. An agreement that Dr. Green shall be held by the United States government as a hostage for Dr. Rucker; other surgeons to be exchanged.

3d. That all officers commanding negro troops, and negro troops themselves, shall be treated as other prisoners of war, and exchanged in the same way. I feel constrained, however, for reasons stated above, to ask for full instructions as soon as possible. You may rest assured that I shall enter into no unauthorized agreement with Mr. Ould, nor shall I discuss with him any point on which I am not fully instructed. I have the honor, also, to forward you the enclosed from Mr. Ould, upon which I should like to have your views before seeing him.

I am, general, very respectfully, your obedient servant,

S. A. MEREDITH,
Brigadier General and Commissioner for Exchange.

Major General E. A. HITCHCOCK,
Washington, D. C.

WASHINGTON CITY, D. C.,
August 13, 1863.

SIR: In answer to your communication of the 7th instant, covering the letter of Mr. Ould, of the 5th instant, I have to enclose for your guidance a memorandum from Major General Halleck, approved by the Secretary of War, containing the decision upon the letter referred to, upon which you can confer with Mr. Ould upon your next interview with him, presenting the proposition as a definite one, without argument on your part.

Should the proposal be accepted with authority, you will only need to make the declaration it contemplates. If it should not be accepted, you will please merely transmit any observations which Mr. Ould may desire to present, for such action as may be determined upon at general headquarters.

Very respectfully, your obedient servant,

E. A. HITCHCOCK,
Major General of Volunteers,
Commissioner for Exchange of Prisoners.

General S. A. MEREDITH, &c., &c.

HEADQUARTERS OF THE ARMY,
Washington, August 12, 1863.

Robert Ould, agent of exchange of prisoners, in his letter of August 5, to Brigadier General S. A. Meredith, claims that the prisoners captured and paroled by the enemy's forces in Maryland and elsewhere, prior to the 3d of July, should either be regarded as legally paroled or returned to the enemy as prisoners of war.

It will be observed that General Order No. 100, current series, simply announces general principles, which apply only in the absence of special agreements. So far from changing in any way the cartel, Lieutenant Colonel Ludlow notified Mr. Ould, at the time of giving him this order, that our government would regard no parole as binding which was not given in conformity with the provisions of the cartel.

This was not only fully understood at the time, but, it is alleged and believed, has been carried out by the enemy whenever it suited his convenience. It is understood that rebel prisoners illegally paroled by our officers have been returned to the ranks without exchange.

In regard to the prisoners paroled in Maryland and Pennsylvania by General Lee and his officers, it is stated by General Meade that General Lee requested him to appoint a place of exchange in accordance with the provisions of the cartel, and that he (General Meade) declined the proposition.

Nevertheless, in order to disembarrass himself from the care of these prisoners General Lee proceeded to parole them. General Lee's officers in receiving these paroles, and our officers and men in giving them, knew or ought to have known that they were utterly null and void. And now, after having released our men on illegal paroles, in order to avoid guarding and feeding them, when his army was hard pressed and retreating before General Meade, General Lee, or rather his agent, Mr. Ould, insists that the United States government shall either respect these illegal paroles, or deliver the persons so paroled to the confederate authorities at City Point.

This is certainly a most extraordinary demand, and cannot be acceded to. In order, however, to avoid any difficulty on this point, General Meredith will be authorized to agree with Mr. Ould, that all paroles given by officers and men on either side, between the 23d of May and the 3d of July, not in conformity with the stipulations of the cartel, be regarded as null and void, a declaration to that effect being published to the armies of both belligerents.

The other three points mentioned in General Meredith's letter of the 7th instant seem to be fully understood by him. The government of the United States will, under no circumstances, yield either of these points.

The foregoing memorandum has been examined and approved by the Secretary of War.

H. W. HALLECK,
General-in-Chief.

Major General HITCHCOCK.

HEADQUARTERS DEPARTMENT OF VIRGINIA,
Fortress Monroe, August 26, 1863.

SIR: Your communication of the 20th instant, in answer to mine of the 19th, in relation to Mr. Daniel Gerhart, is received. No case is known of the detention in the north of a non-combatant, which assimilates to that of Mr. Gerhart in the south. In all cases of the arrest of non-combatants, it has been upon some special causes making it necessary and proper. If there was a disposition north to arrest citizens of the south, merely as such, the positions of the United States forces would show every one that such arrests could be made almost without limit. If you will state a case parallel to that of Mr. Gerhart, I will refer it at once to the proper authority, and it will no doubt be considered with every disposition to afford relief.

Respectfully, your obedient servant,

S. A. MEREDITH,
Brigadier General and Agent of Exchange.

Hon. ROBERT OULD,
Agent of Exchange, Richmond, Va.

CONFEDERATE STATES OF AMERICA,
War Department, Richmond, Virginia, September 7, 1863.

SIR: I confess my great astonishment in not receiving one word from you in reference to the very grave and important matters which were the subjects of discussion between us in our interview at City Point. That interview took place two weeks ago. You stated that you were not prepared to accept or reject the proposition which I then made, but that you would immediately inform your government of its nature, and give me a speedy answer in person or by letter. Though two boats have been despatched from Fortress Monroe to City Point, and two weeks have elapsed since our meeting, no reference or allusion to the subjects of controversy has been made by you. At our interview you told me, in answer to my urgent request, that there should be no delay—that not more than a week would elapse before you would be prepared with your answer. Under these circumstances, if you were not ready, every consideration would seem to demand that some excuse should be furnished or the delay explained. As, however, you do not refer to the matter at all, I am left only to draw the conclusion that you do not intend to give an answer to my proposition. I therefore inform you that the confederate authorities will consider themselves entirely at liberty to pursue any course with reference to my written proposition to you which they may deem right and proper under all the circumstances of the case.

Respectfully, your obedient servant,

ROBERT OULD,
Agent of Exchange.

Brig. General S. A. MEREDITH,
Agent of Exchange.

[Exchange Notice No. 6.]

RICHMOND, *September* 12, 1863.

The following confederate officers and men, captured at Vicksburg, Mississippi, July 4, 1863, and subsequently paroled, have been duly exchanged, and are hereby so declared:

1. The officers and men of General C. L. Stevenson's division.
2. The officers and men of General Bowen's division.
3. The officers and men of Brigadier General Moore's brigade.
4. The officers and men of the 2d Texas regiment.
5. The officers and men of Waul's legion.
6. Also all confederate officers and men who have been delivered at City Point at any time previous to July 25, 1863, have been duly exchanged, and are hereby so declared.

ROBERT OULD,
Agent of Exchange.

HEADQUARTERS DEPARTMENT OF VIRGINIA, 7TH ARMY CORPS,
Fort Monroe, Virginia, September 14, 1863.

SIR: In your letter of September 7, declining to exchange General Graham for General Smith, you state "that I appear to be laboring under some strong mistake; that General Smith has already been exchanged, and that I have received the equivalent." On July 14, 1863, my predecessor, Lieutenant Colonel Ludlow, wrote to you, positively declining to unite with you in your declaration of exchange of July 13, and requesting you to notify the officers therein named that their exchange would not be recognized by the authorities of the United States. May I ask who was the equivalent delivered for General Smith? I now repeat to you the notification of Lieutenant Colonel Ludlow, and state that the authorities of the United States will not recognize the exchange of the above officers until united in by me.

Respectfully, your obedient servant,

S. A. MEREDITH.
Brig. Gen., Com'r for Exchange.

Hon. ROBERT OULD,
Agent of Exchange.

CONFEDERATE STATES OF AMERICA,
War Department, Richmond, Virginia, September 14, 1863.

SIR: In your letter of the 14th instant you inquired " who was the equivalent delivered for General Smith." If you will refer to my letters of the 13th and 17th of July you will find out the equivalent. It had been our practice, whenever a special exchange was declared by one party, to allow the other to select the equivalent from prisoners already paroled or delivered. I pursued that course in the case of the Vicksburg general officers. The equivalent could be found in officers and men paroled at Fredericksburg, in pursuance of an agreement between Generals Lee and Hooker. If that was not satisfactory, the equivalent could easily be found in the ten thousand prisoners whom I had released from captivity and sent to City Point. In that ten thousand there was an excess of more than six thousand at least over the number you had delivered at the same place since the last general declaration of exchange. My letter of the 17th of July, contains a fair statement not only of the practice of the agents of exchange, but of the grounds of my authority to declare the exchange of the Vicksburg general officers, including General M. L. Smith. The efforts to cast discredit upon the regular and honorable exchange of these officers is, to use a phrase of your own in one of your letters of the 14th instant," simply ridiculous."

Respectfully, your obedient servant,

ROBERT OULD,
Agent of Exchange.

Brig. General S. A. MEREDITH,
Agent of Exchange.

WASHINGTON CITY, D. C., *September* 18, 1863.

SIR: Your communication of the 14th instant to Colonel Hoffman, enclosing the letter of Mr. Ould of the 11th, is before me.

For the purpose of guarding against a misunderstanding, and an erroneous principle of action on the subject of declaring exchanges, you will inform Mr. Ould that the ex parte declaration of exchange, proposed in his communication to be made the next day, (following the date of that communication,) is deemed to be not only without authority from the cartel, but contrary to the usages of war.

The 5th article of the cartel (General Orders No. 142, 1862) would have authorized Mr. Ould to discharge prisoners of the federal forces, furnishing a list of them, and then to discharge an equal number of his own officers and men from parole. The cartel not only contemplates a mutual exchange of lists, (article 5,) but expressly declares (article 4) that no exchange is to be considered complete until the officer or soldier exchanged for has been actually restored to the lines to which he belongs.

In order to complete the arrangement declared by Mr. Ould, it will be necessary for you to make a declaration of exchange of as many of our officers and men as have been delivered at City Point since the last declaration, provided the number does not exceed the number designated in Mr. Ould's declaration.

Then you can proceed further, and arrange with Mr. Ould for the discharge from parole of any excess which can be balanced either way by officers or soldiers actually on parole. Prisoners of war actually in our hands are not to be exchanged at the present time. You will please be careful not to jeopard this point. You can receive any officers or soldiers whom Mr. Ould may offer at City Point, and arrange with him for a mutual declaration of exchange for those of his officers and men already on parole in the south, grade for grade.

Colonel Hoffman's letter of the 5th ultimo will give you some suggestions about exchanges, but it will be necessary for you to be exceedingly guarded in framing your declaration to confine its application to rebel prisoners already paroled, and on no account, by any accident, to use language which can give the south a claim upon prisoners now in our actual possession; not but that these will be used for exchange at the proper time, but not while the north has, already delivered and on parole, more than enough to cover all deliveries made or to be made by the south.

Very respectfully, your obedient servant,
E. A. HITCHCOCK,
Major General Volunteers, Commissioner of Exchange.
General S. A. MEREDITH,
Commissioner for Exchanges.

HEADQUARTERS DEPARTMENT OF VIRGINIA,
Fortress Monroe, August 25, 1863.

GENERAL: I have just returned from a meeting with the rebel agent of exchange at City Point, and I have the honor to report to you that, in reply to his letter to me, dated August 5, 1863, wherein he claims "that the prisoners captured and paroled by the rebel forces in Maryland and elsewhere prior to the third of July should either be regarded as legally paroled, or returned as prisoners of war," I made the following proposition, as directed in the letter of the general-in-chief to you of August 12, 1863:

"CITY POINT, VIRGINIA, *August 24. 1863.*

"I propose, on behalf of the government of the United States, that all paroles given by officers and men between the 23d day of May, 1863, and the 3d day of July, 1863, not in conformity with the stipulations of the cartel, shall be regarded as null and void, a declaration to this effect to be published to both armies.

"S. A. MEREDITH,
"*Brigadier General and Commissioner for Exchanges.*"

This was declined, and the following was offered by Mr. Ould:

"CITY POINT, *August* 24, 1864.

"I propose that all paroles on both sides heretofore given shall be determined by the General Orders issued by the War Department of the United States, to wit, No. 49, No. 100, and No. 207 of this year, according to their respective dates, and in conformity with paragraph 131 of General Order No. 100, so long as said paragraph was in force. If this proposition is not acceptable, I propose that the practice heretofore adopted, respecting paroles and exchanges, be continued. In other words, I propose that the whole question of paroles be determined by the General Orders of the United States, according to their dates, or that it be decided by former practice.

"ROBERT OULD,
"*Agent of Exchange.*"

In reply to my demand for the release of Colonel Streight and his command, I was informed that they were in Richmond held as other prisoners of war, and will be exchanged when exchanges of officers are resumed. In relation to Dr. Rucker, Mr. Ould referred me to his letter of August 16, which I have the honor to forward herewith.

To my demand "that all officers commanding negro troops, and negro troops themselves, should be treated as other prisoners of war, and be exchanged a such," Mr. Ould declined acceding, remarking that they (the rebels) would "die in the last ditch" before giving up the right to send slaves back to slavery as property recaptured; but that they were willing to make exceptions in the case of *free* blacks. He could not exactly tell me how his authorities intended to distinguish between the two, (free and slave,) but presumed that evidence as to the fact of freedom would be taken into consideration. As their laws put slave and free upon the same footing, no comment is necessary.

An informal proposition was made to the following effect: "To exchange officer for officer of the same grade, except such as are in command of negro troops," which was declined.

Mr. Ould expresses a willingness to release all chaplains, provided that one Septimus Cameron, who, he stated, had been in prison for a year, should be released, or indicted for any offence he may have committed. On my inquiring about and urging the release of the members of the sanitary commission, I was informed that they would be set free on making a statement in writing that they had, at any time, been of assistance to rebel soldiers. General Neal Dow has been handed over to the governor of Alabama; Lieutenant Colonel Powell is in Libby prison, Richmond. I have notified the rebel authorities in relation to the two above-named officers, as directed in yours of the 18th ultimo.

The rebel authorities wish to continue exchanging non-commissioned officers and privates as usual, returning as many as we send.

I have given you, I believe, the substance of all that took place, according to your suggestion. I avoided much discussion. No agreement as to exchanges was arrived at.

I am, general, very respectfully, your obedient servant,
S. A. MEREDITH,
Brigadier General and Commissioner for Exchange.

Major General E. A. HITCHCOCK,
Commissioner for Exchange of Prisoners, Washington City, D. C.

WASHINGTON CITY, D. C,
September 21, 1863.

The communication of the 3d instant from his excellency the governor of Connecticut, on the subject of the crew of the bark Texana, having been returned with an indorsement from Mr. Ould, proposing to discharge said crew "on the release of those similarly situated in federal prisons," you are requested to say to Mr. Ould that I do not know nor can I hear of any prisoners held by us under circumstances corresponding to those of the Texana held in the south. If Mr. Ould will refer specifically to any such prisoners in our hands, they shall be released—it being understood that the cases shall be similar.

The communication from Mr. Ould of the 1st of August, referred to in the indorsement as unanswered, was handed to the Secretary of War on its receipt, who does not think proper to enter into such broad general agreements as proposed, implying so settled a state of things as does not in fact exist.

Very respectfully your obedient servant,
E. A. HITCHCOCK,
Major General Volunteers, Commissioner
for Exchange of Prisoners.

General S. A. MEREDITH,
Commissioner for Exchange of Prisoners.

HEADQUARTERS DEPARTMENT OF VIRGINIA,
Fort Monroe, September 23, 1863.

SIR: I have the honor to report to you herewith the result of my interview with the rebel agent of exchange. I called his attention to the fact that his declaration of exchange of the 12th instant was not in accordance with the terms of the cartel; he acknowledged it to be the case, but stated that such had been the practice heretofore between Lieut. Col. Ludlow and himself, and that when one agent declared a special exchange, the other was allowed to select the equivalents; this he expressed a desire that I should do. I expressed my readiness to complete the arrangement which he had "declared," but this could not be consummated, in consequence of the rebel agent's claiming as valid the paroles at Gettysburg and elsewhere, amounting to some 4,800.

Mr. Ould made the following proposition: "That all officers and men on both sides be released, unless there be actual charges against them. If officers or men are held on charges which their government consider unjust, let one or more hostages be held for such. If there be charges against officers and men, and they are not tried on the same within a reasonable time, (to be agreed upon,) they are to be discharged.

I am, general, very respectfully, your obedient servant.

S. A. MEREDITH,
Brigadier General and Commissioner for Exchange.

Major General E. A. HITCHCOCK,
Commissioner for Exchanges, Washington, D. C.

HEADQUARTERS DEPARTMENT OF VIRGINIA,
Fort Monroe, September 24, 1863.

SIR: To meet your declaration of exchange of the 12th instant, I inform you that I have this day announced the following:

"A declaration of exchange having been announced by R. Ould, esq., agent for exchange, at Richmond, Virginia, dated September 12, 1863, to meet the same, in part, as equivalents, it is hereby declared that all officers and men of the United States army captured and paroled at any time previous to the 1st September, 1863, are duly exchanged."

The number of officers covered by the first five sections of your declaration is	1,208	
The number of enlisted men is		14,865
The number of officers covered by 6th section is	72	
The number of enlisted men is		8,014
Making a total of officers	1,280	
And total of enlisted men	22,879	
Aggregate	24,159	
Reduced to enlisted men		29,433
Of the federal troops on parole, there are officers	76	
Enlisted men	19,083	
Aggregate	19,159	
Reduced to enlisted men		19,409
Which gives a balance in our favor of		10,024

I now claim this balance which is due us, and I demand that you return to their paroles all officers and men for whom you have paroled no equivalents, or that you release an equal number from the prisons in Richmond.

Your declaration was wholly unwarranted under the cartel, and it might, with great propriety, be set aside. In it you failed to announce to me the 6th section, as published in the Richmond Enquirer of the 10th instant, which covers 72 officers, and 8,014 enlisted men. You did not, according to the terms of the cartel, furnish me with any "list," or even give me the number of men, by which I could declare equivalents, nor did you give me any time to prepare my announcement. I here deem it incumbent upon me to state that I consider your course in this matter a deliberate breach of good faith on the part of the authorities under whom you act. The 5th article of the cartel (General Orders No. 142, 1862) would have authorized you to discharge prisoners of the federal forces, furnishing a "list" of them, and then you could have discharged an equal number of your own officers and men "from parole." The cartel not only contemplates a "mutual" exchange of "lists," (article 5,) but expressly declares (article 4) that no exchange is to be considered complete, until the officer or soldier exchanged for has been actually restored to the lines to which he belongs.

As to the paroles given at Gettysburg and elsewhere, you made an agreement with my predecessor, Lieutenant Colonel Ludlow, to take effect from May 22, 1863, that all paroles given, not in accordance with the cartel, should be considered null and void. How, then, can you claim as valid the Gettysburg paroles?

If you have any rolls or lists of any men whom you may have paroled that I have not given you credit for, or if there should be any errors in my account, I will be happy to rectify the same.

You declared exchanged, before my predecessor was relieved, certain officers captured at Vicksburg, in which declaration he refused to unite. There are but two officers, I believe, (Generals Stevenson and Bowen,) who are covered by your declaration of the 12th instant. If the other officers named have not been returned to their paroles, as requested by Lieutenant Colonel Ludlow, you are indebted to us for their equivalents. The chief ground of the objection to that declaration is, that at that time there were no equivalents of the same grade in our possession, (the only condition which would have warranted your making the declaration,) and if we consented to it, we would be obliged to offset them by officers of inferior rank.

In making up the number of federal troops to be exchanged, I have included all those mustered out of the service, all discharged, deserted and deceased.

Respectfully, your obedient servant,

S. A. MEREDITH,
Brigadier General and Commissioner for Exchange.

Hon. R. Ould,
Agent of Exchange, Richmond, Virginia.

WASHINGTON CITY, D. C., *September* 26, 1863.

SIR: The proposition submitted as from Mr. Ould, in your letter of the 22d instant, "that all officers and men on both sides be released, unless there be actual charges against them," &c., is not accepted. The effort to make a distinction between officers serving with different species of troops can receive no countenance whatever.

The existing cartel is sufficient to meet all the demands of the laws of war.
Very respectfully, your obedient servant,

E. A. HITCHCOCK,
Major General of Volunteers, &c.

General S. A. MEREDITH,
Commissioner for the Exchange of Prisoners.

RICHMOND, *October* 2, 1863.

SIR: Your communication of the 24th ultimo, declaring that "all officers and men of the United States army captured and paroled at any time previous to the 1st of September, 1863, are duly exchanged," has been received.

You are aware that when I met you, on the 24th of August last, at City Point, I made to you the following proposal, to wit: "I propose that all paroles on both sides heretofore given shall be determined by the General Orders issued by the War Department of the United States, to wit, No. 49, No. 100, and No. 207, of this year, according to their respective dates, and in conformity with paragraph 131 of General Order No. 100, so long as said paragraph was in force. If this proposition is not acceptable, I propose that the practice heretofore adopted respecting paroles and exchanges be continued. In other words, I propose that the whole question of paroles be determined by the General Orders of the United States, according to dates, or that it be decided by former practice." You have neither accepted nor declined either branch of that proposal, although I have, both in personal interview and by letter, solicited you to do one or the other. On the same day you submitted to me your proposition, which, unlike mine, was prepared beforehand, and which is as follows: "I propose, on behalf of the government of the United States, that all paroles given by officers and men between the 23d day of May, 1863, and the 3d day of July, 1863, not in conformity with the stipulations of the cartel, shall be regarded as null and void. A declaration to this effect to be published to both armies." That proposition I immediately declined. I then and there gave you my reasons. In the first place, I informed you that the confederate authorities had never at any time, and did not then, ask that paroles "not in conformity with the stipulations of the cartel" should be regarded as valid. I further told you that an agreement to regard "as null and void" paroles between certain dates, which were "not in conformity with the stipulations of the cartel," was an implication that paroles liable to the same objection before the first-named date, and after the last, *should* be regarded as valid, and was, therefore, necessarily vicious on its very face. I also told you that another reason for declining your proposition was the one which caused you to make it, to wit: That the paroles which had been given to us were *between* the dates embraced in your proposition, while those given to you were before and after. When I made the objection to your proposal that it intimated that paroles "not in conformity with the stipulations of the cartel," before the 23d of May, and after the 3d of July of this year, were to be regarded as valid, I asked you to state in writing that no such intimation was conveyed. This you declined to do, saying somewhat brusquely that you did not wish to have any discussion about the matter. Upon my pressing the subject, however, you put a memorandum at the foot of the proposition, saying that the proposal was in reply to my letter of August 5, 1863, and in lieu of the proposition therein made by me. You would not, did not, disclaim the implication which your proposition contained, nor have you done so since. My letter of the 5th of August only demanded, in compliance with your own General Order No. 100, that if you rejected the paroles, the parties should be delivered to us. You informed me that you would transmit my proposition to Washington, and give me a speedy answer in person or by letter.

On the 7th of September I complained that no reply had been returned, although two weeks had elapsed and two boats had been despatched to City Point since the date of our interview. At the same time I informed you that the confederate authorities would consider themselves entirely at liberty to pursue any course with reference to my proposition which they might deem right and proper under all the circumstances of the case.

Accordingly, on the 11th of September, in pursuance of this plain intimation, I notified you that on the following day (that being the time when the notice would reach you) I would declare exchanged a portion of the Vicksburg captures. I gave you the divisions, brigades, regiments, and batteries. I also informed you that I had in my possession more valid paroles of your officers and men than would be an equivalent for the exchange I then declared; that, in addition, I had delivered at City Point some ten or twelve thousand men since the last declaration of exchange; that as it had been the practice, however, of the agents of exchange whenever one of them declared a special exchange to allow the other to select the equivalents, I gave you that privilege, and if you did not avail yourself of it I would name the federal officers and men who were discharged from their parole by reasons of the declaration of exchange then made. This notification to you was not only in accordance with former practice, but was sanctioned, if not demanded, by the fifth article of the cartel, which, after providing for the manner in which "each party" may discharge "their" officers and men from parole, says, "thus enabling *each* party to relieve from parole such of *their own* officers and men as the party may choose." I have said this course was in accordance with former practice, and for proof refer you to the letters of Lieutenant Colonel Ludlow, former agent of exchange, of the following dates of this year, to wit: April 6, 8, 13, 19, and 27, May 12, 26, and 30, June 5, 9, and 13, wherein he declared the exchange of federal officers and men. In one of Lieutenant Colonel Ludlow's communications of May 30, 1863, he says, "I have declared exchanged the Holly Springs capture; the ninety-first regiment Illinois volunteers, captured at Elizabethtown, Kentucky, December 27, 1862, and the captures at Mount Sterling on the 22d and 23d of March, 1863, also the officers and men of the Indianola. The exact numbers I have not on hand, but they foot up some hundreds less than the balance due. I will furnish you with the exact numbers as soon as received." The same boat that conveyed that communication brought another written subsequently, but dated the same day, as follows: "I have declared exchanged the fifty-first (51st) regiment Indiana volunteers, seventy-third (73d) regiment Indiana volunteers, and third regiment Ohio volunteers. These number each less than three hundred men, and compose a part of Streight's brigade. I will add to the above declaration the eightieth regiment Illinois volunteers, and fifty-eight (58) men of the first Tennessee cavalry."

The enlisted men alone, designated in *either one* of the communications, exceeded the "balance" due to Lieutenant Colonel Ludlow. The excess in both communications was 2,290, without taking into account "the captures at Mount Sterling on the 22d and 23d of March, 1863."

You will observe that Lieutenant Colonel Ludlow, in these two communications, did not furnish me with "any list, or even give me the number of men, by which I could declare equivalents, nor did he give me any time to prepare my announcement." I quote from your letter of the 24th of September to me. Not only was that the case, but he made a wholesale exchange of the Mount Sterling capture by a simple reference to it as being made on the 22d and 23d of March, 1863, without any designation of corps, division, brigade, regiment, or company. Further than that, I have never to this day been furnished with a list of those captured at Mount Sterling, or even with the aggregate number.

Such, then, were the circumstances, and such the precedents, under which I declared the exchange of September 12, 1863. I have purposely gone into minute and faithful detail in consequence of the extraordinary character of your letter of the 24th of September. You state that you consider my course to be a deliberate breach of good faith on the part of the authorities under whom I act. In a bungling sort of way you have used language which casts an offensive aspersion both upon myself and the government I represent. If there had not been subjects of very grave import to both people referred to in other portions of your communication, I would have treated it with the silent contempt it deserved, and returned it to you without comment. For the first time in the correspondence of the agents of exchange has any such discourtesy occurred. I regret it very much. Heretofore I have had occasion to complain of the action of your government, but it has always been done with decorum. I have never written a word personally offensive to the federal agent of exchange, or insulted his government with a charge of "*deliberate* breach of good faith." It is a matter of very little moment to me what may be your opinion of "my course." There are some people connected with this war who, either from ignorance or passion, seem to have no clear ideas on any subject. The opinion of such, even if uttered in the language of courtesy, is but of little avail, but if expressed with intemperance, only "exalts their folly." There has been no breach of faith on the part of the Confederate States, "deliberate" or otherwise. You were importuned to agree to some fair principle by which paroles could be adjusted and computed. After patient waiting—after failure on your part to respond affirmatively or negatively—the confederate government, through its agent of exchange, did what was demanded by courtesy, and justified both by former practice and the provisions of the cartel.

I now proceed to notice the misstatements of your letter. I will not call them "deliberate," although you had the means of correcting them at your hands, for such phraseology, so open to the imputation of discourtesy and coarseness, finds in such communications as the present only the precedent of your example.

1. Your computation of paroles is incorrect on both sides. As to your item of 1,208 officers and 14,865 men, embraced by the first five sections of my exchange notice, I have no exception to make. Some of our Vicksburg rolls were lost, and I have not the means of making an accurate computation as to them. Your second item, however, of 72 officers and 8,014 men, embracing the sixth section of my exchange notice, is incorrect. In the first place, all the officers *on both sides*, who have been delivered at City Point, are exchanged. They were specially exchanged. Major Mulford knows that fact. All confederate soldiers who were delivered at City Point up to May 23, 1863, including said date, were declared exchanged by Lieut. Colonel Ludlow, while the federal troops were only exchanged up to May 6, 1863. The number of confederate soldiers reduced to privates, delivered at City Point from May 23 to July 25, (the date named in my notice,) is 5,881, instead of 8,014. The rolls show this very clearly. Of the federal troops on parole, you say there are 76 officers and 19,083 men. If these officers are those delivered at City Point, you make an error against yourself. They have been exchanged. From the 6th of May, 1863, (the time of the last exchange of federal troops) to the 1st of September, 1863, (the time named in your notice) I have delivered at City Point alone, in privates, 18,610. All of these are on parole. I have other valid paroles in my possession, amounting to at least 16,000 more. Allowing, therefore, that your Vicksburg computation is correct, you owe me upon the last notice which you have published more than 7,000, instead of my owing you 10,024, as you claim. Many of the 16,000 paroles to which I have referred have been acknowledged by Lieut. Colonel Ludlow in his correspondence. So much as to your computation, and your exchange notice based upon it.

2. You say I failed to announce to you "the sixth section of my exchange notice, as published in the Richmond Enquirer of the 10th instant, which covers 72 officers and 8,014 enlisted men." This is not so. On the 1st of August last I informed you in writing that I had declared exchanged all confederate soldiers who had been delivered at City Point, up to July 20, 1863. No deliveries were made at City Point between July 20 and July 25, and therefore one announcement was the same as the other. I did not inform you of the exchange of the City Point men in my letter of the 11th of September, because I had already notified you on the first of August.

3. You say I did not furnish you with any list, or even give the number of men, by which you could declare equivalents, nor did I give you any time to prepare your announcement. You were furnished with the lists of all paroled men delivered at City Point, numbering, up to September 1, 18,610 men. As to other paroles held by me, you failed to accept or decline the terms upon which they were to be computed and adjusted, and therefore it was useless to send them. You had, or ought to have had, duplicates of many of them in your possession. If there was any particular capture on parole, or any special class of paroled men whom you wished to declare exchanged, you had only to announce that fact, and the lists would be furnished, if I had them and you had not. With what propriety could I send you lists which I believed to be in accordance with the cartel, but which you intimated you would decline to acknowledge? Moreover, according to my interpretation of the cartel, that instrument very clearly gives the right to you to select what federal officers and men shall be relieved from their parole, whenever I discharge our officers and men from their parole. I claim the same right when you declare an exchange of your paroled men. If I had sent you lists of such of your officers and men as were relieved from their parole by my declaration of exchange, I would in effect have violated that provision of the cartel which gives the right to "each party to relieve from parole such of their own officers and men as the party may choose." It was entirely unnecessary for me to give you the number of men whom my notice declared exchanged. They were all Vicksburg captures, or City Point deliveries. You had the rolls of both. You had in your possession as much information as I could communicate, even if I had held the Vicksburg rolls, which I did not. I have already proved to you by the record that the former federal agent, when he declared exchanges, gave neither lists nor the number of men. There is, however, a more recent case. You yourself have just declared a sweeping exchange. You have not furnished me with any lists or designation of corps, division, brigade, regiment, or company, notwithstanding the clamor you have raised about my omission in those particulars. Your objection as to want of time for the preparation of your announcement is a small one at best. The cartel does not make it incumbent upon me to give you time. Your predecessor did not give it to me. The correspondence, however, between us, before the 12 of September, was of such a nature as must have prevented a surprise.

4. I did not make any such agreement with your predecessor, Lieut. Colonel Ludlow, as you state, nor did I ever make any agreement with any one, by which I renounced the right to claim the paroles given at Gettysburg. The first official letter which I ever addressed to you was in relation to this very subject. It bears date August 1, 1863, and is as follows:

"SIR: In the 'Army and Navy Official Gazette,' of the date of July 14, 1863, I find a letter of Lieut. Colonel Ludlow, of the date of July 7, 1863, addressed to Colonel J. C. Kelton. In it is the following paragraph, to wit:

"'I have the honor also to state that, since the 22d of May last, it has been distinctly understood between Mr. Ould and myself that all captures must be reduced to possession, and that all paroles are to be disregarded, unless taken under the special arrangement of commanding officers of armies in the field, as prescribed in section seven of the cartel.'

"If Lieut. Colonel Ludlow means that he had declared to me that such was the rule which had been adopted by the United States, in relation to captures and paroles, to go into effect from and after May 23, 1863, he is entirely right. If he means that I, at any time, consented to adopt or acquiesce in any such rule, he is entirely wrong. All that passed between us on that subject is in writing. The correspondence will interpret itself.

"Respectfully, your obedient servant,

"ROBERT OULD,
"*Agent of Exchange.*

"Brigadier General S. A. MEREDITH,
"*Agent of Exchange.*"

The General Order No. 100, issued at Washington, which Lieut. Colonel Ludlow communicated to me on the 23d of May, 1863, in its 131st paragraph provides that "if the government does not approve of the parole, the paroled officer must return into captivity, and should the enemy refuse to receive him he is free of his parole." In no communication, in no interview with either Lieut. Colonel Ludlow or yourself, where the subject was under consideration, did I ever fail to demand that if your government rejected the paroles the parties should return into captivity. I had the warrant of your own general order for that demand, but pleaded it in vain. So far from carrying out its own general order, your government, on the 30th of June last, while the order was in force, and before the publication of General Order No. 207, convened a court of inquiry, and required the court to give its opinion on the following point, to wit: whether Major Duane and Captain Michler, captured and paroled on the 28th of June, 1863, should be placed on duty without exchange, or be required to return to the enemy as prisoners of war. The general order required the latter, but the court found that the government was free to place those officers on duty without exchange. The reason given by the court was not that the federal agent and myself had *agreed* to regard such paroles as invalid, but that I had been *notified* they would not be recognized. It is true that I was informed that certain paroles would not be considered as valid, but I was also notified at the same time, by the same hand and through the same instrument, that the "paroled officer" must return into captivity if his parole was not approved. In other words, on that day, May 23, 1863, Lieut. Colonel Ludlow, with little or no comment, delivered to me General Order No. 100 as the rules adopted for the government of the federal army. I never had any intimation that all the provisions of Generel Order No. 100 did not continue in force, until I received, on the 8th of July, 1863, the following letter from Lieut. Colonel Ludlow:

"FORT MONROE, *July* 7, 1863.

"SIR: I herewith enclose to you a copy of General Order No. 207, which contains some additional provisions to those mentioned in my communication to you of the 22d of May last. It is understood that officers of the United States and confederate officers have, at various times and places, paroled and released prisoners of war not in accordance with the cartel.

"The government of the United States will not recognize, and will not expect the confederate authorities to recognize, such unauthorized paroles. 'Prisoners released on parole, not authorized by the cartel, after my notice to you of the 22d of May, will not be regarded as prisoners of war, and will not be exchanged.'

"When prisoners of war have been released without the delivery specified in the cartel since the 22d of May last, such release will be regarded as unconditional, and the prisoners released as subject to orders without exchange, the same as if they had never been captured.

"I am, very respectfully, your obedient servant,
"WILLIAM H. LUDLOW,
"*Lieutenant Colonel and Agent for Exchange of Prisoners.*
"Hon. ROBERT OULD,
"*Agent for Exchange of Prisoners.*"

The "notice" referred to in Lieutenant Colonel Ludlow's letter was the delivery of General Order No. 100, with its 131st paragraph. That paragraph was set aside by the provisions of General Order No. 207, which bears date July 3, 1863, three days *after* the submission of the question of the paroles of Duane and Michler to the court of inquiry, two days *after* its finding, and several days *after* our captures in the Gettysburg campaign. On the 7th of July, 1863, Lieutenant Colonel Ludlow substantially informs me that, although he notified me, on the 22d of May, that paragraph 131 of General Order No. 100 was to be and continue in force; yet, under the circumstances of the case, and in view of what had taken place in Maryland and Pennsylvania, said paragraph was not to be considered as being in force at any time after the 22d of May, and General Order No. 207, although it was issued July 3, 1863, should be construed as bearing date the 22d of May preceding.

It will be observed that Lieutenant Colonel Ludlow, in his letter to me of the 7th of July, nowhere says I had made any agreement with him, and yet it bears the same date as his letter to Colonel Kelton. It is apparent on the face of the paper that he is conveying to me certain information for the first time, and that this information is the "additional provisions" of General Order No. 207, one of which set aside paragraph 131 of General Orders No. 100. The court of inquiry in its finding, (see Army and Navy Officers' Gazette, July 14, 1863,) says I was "*notified*," &c. Lieutenant Colonel Ludlow, in his letter to Colonel Kelton, says it was distinctly "*understood*" between Mr. Ould and himself, &c. You, in your letter of the 24th of September, say I made an "*agreement*" with your predecessor. The notification first rises to an understanding, and is then elevated into an agreement. What further promotion it will receive, remains to be seen.

You have charged a deliberate breach of good faith upon the part of the Confederate States. Let me bring to your attention an incident connected with this matter of release from paroles. On March 9, 1863, General Schenck, of immortal memory, issued a General Order No. 15, requiring all officers and men who had been captured and paroled in his department, and particularly in the Shenandoah valley, but who had not been exchanged, to return to duty on penalty of being considered deserters. Your General Order in force at that time—No. 49, February 28, 1863—in section 8, provided, that if the engagement which a prisoner made was not approved by his government, he was bound to return and surrender himself as a prisoner of war. The same General Order No. 49, in the same section 8, uses these memorable words, which I now set up against your present extraordinary claims, to wit: "His own government cannot at the same time disown his engagement and refuse his return as a prisoner." In spite of those honest words General Schenck issued his order, which, to this day, has not been countermanded; in effect, directing not only that such as were captured and paroled after March 9, 1863, should return to duty, but also all who had been captured and paroled under the circumstances named, since the beginning of hostilities, on penalty of being considered deserters.

At that very time, and afterwards, even to as late as Stoneman's raid, the former agent of exchange was charging against me and receiving credit for captures and paroles similar to those repudiated by Schenck's order. It is due to Lieutenant Colonel Ludlow that I should say, that when the matter was brought to his attention, he declared that Schenck's action was without proper authority, and that I would have credit for such as reported for duty under the order. Still the order was not countermanded, but, on the contrary, has been followed and sustained by General Order No. 207. I have received no returns of such as have reported under Schenck's order, and never will.

In your letter of the 24th of September, and others, you refer, in connexion with our Gettysburg captures, to "paroles not in accordance with the cartel." The phrase figures not only in your correspondence, but in the findings of your courts, and in some of your general orders. Let me here, in the most formal manner, assure you that the confederate government considers the cartel to be binding and imperative to the fullest extent of any and all of its provisions. I have never asked you to respect a parole which is inconsistent with that instrument. You say the Gettysburg paroles are in contravention of the cartel. Let me give you some of them—all or nearly all of them belong to one or the other class :

"I, the subscriber, a prisoner of war, captured near Gettysburg, Pennsylvania, do give my parole of honor not to take up arms against the Confederate States, or to do any military duty whatever, or to give any information that may be prejudicial to the interests of the same, until regularly exchanged. In the event that this parole is not recognized by the federal authorities, I give my parole of honor to report to Richmond, Virginia, as a prisoner of war within thirty (30) days.
"JOHN E. PARSONS,
"*First Lieutenant and Adjutant* 149*th Pennsylvania Volunteers.*"

"I, the subscriber, a prisoner of war, captured near Gettysburg, Pennsylvania, do give my parole of honor not to take up arms against the Confederate States, or to do any military duty whatever, or to give any information that may be prejudicial to the interests of the same, until regularly exchanged. This parole is unconditional, and extended to a wounded officer for the sake of humanity, to save a painful and tedious journey to the rear.
"ROY STOWE,
"*Colonel* 149*th Pennsylvania Volunteers.*"

"We, the undersigned, of the company and regiment opposite our names, do solemnly swear that we will not take up arms against the Confederate States of America until regularly exchanged, in accordance with the cartel, even if required to do so by our government."

"The following named prisoners captured near Gettysburg, Pennsylvania, are paroled on the following conditions, namely: not to take up arms against the Confederate States, or do any military duty whatever, or to give any information that may be prejudicial to the same, until regularly exchanged. This parole is unconditional, and if not recognized by the authorities of the United States government, all pledge themselves to repair to Richmond, as prisoners of war, at the expiration of twenty (20) days from this date."

Does the cartel contemplate that these officers and men should be returned to duty without exchange? It nowhere says so upon its face. When we were without any cartel, all such paroles, and in fact all military paroles, were respected. The very first act of the agents of exchange was to adjust mutual accounts as to the officers and men who had been captured and paroled before the cartel was signed. If it had been intended by the cartel to repudiate such paroles as were given at Gettysburg, or upon any battle-field, a provision to that effect in distinct terms would have been incorporated in it. That instrument was intended to apply to "all prisoners of war held by either party"—to such as were in military depots or prisons—to such as had been removed from the battle-field or place of capture and reduced into actual possession. It left the force and effect of military paroles and the respect which should be paid to them, to be determined by the usages of civilized nations of modern times. It certainly did not purpose to prevent a wounded officer or man from entering into a stipulation not to take up arms until exchanged, as the condition of his release when his life would be at the serious risk of forfeit if he did not make the contract. Nor does it anywhere deny the right of any soldier, wounded or not, to bind his government by his military obligation, when he is in the hands of the enemy. The latter part of article 7 does not really controvert this view. That clause intended to give " the commanders of two opposing armies " the power of declaring an exchange of prisoners, with its further right of paroling whatever surplus there might be after the exchange was arranged. Without such clause, the two commanders would have no right to declare an exchange. It was therefore inserted. Until recently nobody ever pretended that the cartel forbid the giving and receiving of ordinary military paroles. The uniform practice under the cartel for nearly a year sanctioned them. Whatever, however, may be the determination as to this matter, it is entirely clear that at the time the Gettysburg paroles were given, your own military law required that if the parole was not approved, the party should return to our lines. Many of the paroles indicate on their face that the persons giving them were aware of that fact. I have therefore demanded that if you reject these paroles, the parties who gave them should be returned to us. The question between us is not so much whether you will regard these paroles as valid, as whether you will comply with a rule of your own making, and which was advertised to us as being the controlling law of the case.

I know not what you mean by your reference on your third page to article 4 of the cartel. All the officers and men whom I declared exchanged were "actually restored to our lines." All of the officers and men whom I requested you to select as equivalents for them in the exchange, " had been restored to your lines." The parties whom I have declared exchanged have not been " returned to their paroles as requested by Lieutenant Colonel Ludlow." I do not understand by what sort of reading of the exchange notice of the 12th of September you make out that only "two officers (Generals Stevenson and Bowen") were exchanged. My letters of July 13, September 11, and Septemtember 26, will inform you of all the Vicksburg prisoners, officers and men, whom I have declared exchanged.

Your objection to the declaration of the exchange of the general officers paroled at Vicksburg, because there were no equivalents of the same grade, is exploded by the provision of the cartel which declares "that men and officers of lower grades may be exchanged for officers of a higher grade."

I have thus answered all the items of your letter of the 24th of September. I regret the extreme length of the reply. I have, however, confined myself to the matter of that letter, and to such subjects as were directly connected with its contents. In a future communication I will call to your attention the instances of the violation of the cartel by the federal authorities. Notwithstanding the expression of their sudden regard for that instrument, I will show they have continued those violations from its date to the present moment. I, now inform you, in view of the recent declaration of exchange made by you coupled with your failure either to agree to or decline the proposition made to you on the 24th of August last in relation to paroles, that the confederate authorities will consider themselves entirely at liberty to pursue any course as to exchange or paroles which they may deem right and proper under all the circumstances of the case. At the same time I am directed to express their entire willingness to adopt any fair, just, and reciprocal rule in relation to those subjects without any delay.

Respectfully, your obedient servant,

ROBERT OULD,
Agent of Exchange.

Brigadier General S. A. MEREDITH,
Agent of Exchange.

WASHINGTON CITY, D. C.,
October 2, 1863.

SIR: Colonel Hoffman has just shown me another "declaration of exchange' made by Mr. Ould, in which you do not appear to have been consulted.

This mode of *ex parte* declarations is altogether inexplicable, being without warrant from any recognized authority, and may lead to unpleasant consequences to the parties declared thus exchanged if again taken prisoners, the nature of which cannot now be determined.

On the subject of the crew of the Texana, please see the indorsement upon your last report on the subject, forwarded by mail to-day.

In your conferences with Mr. Ould on the subject, you can explain that his propositions are not rejected contumaciously, but simply because there are complications in the matter which make it inexpedient to make a general declaration— one circumstance being, that among the prisoners in our hands a considerable number seem to dread nothing so much as being sent south. In many instances they declare a northern prison their choice in preference to being exchanged.

On this account, I wish you to obtain from Mr. Ould, if you can, a *margin*, so that we can, if we have them, make up the required number without taking active *crews*.

It is hoped that the proposal for an exchange of medical officers and hospital attendants will lead to good results, and that chaplains will also be exchanged.

Mr. Ould's statement of the case of Spencer Kellogg, taking the facts to be as he states them, would appear to be satisfactory, though extremely painful, except that so far as his having been a spy before he was captured, is not regarded as an offence to be punished after being captured.

This principle is so laid down in the "code" we published a few months since. But if Kellogg was a deserter, his fate followed the offence of desertion.

I wish it were possible to obtain the release of Doctor Rucker. The belief is universal on this side that he is not legitimately held. Make another trial in his behalf and that of Doctor Greene, whose fate is bound up with that of Doctor Rucker.

Very respectfully, your obedient servant,
E. A. HITCHCOCK,
Major General of Volunteers, Comm'r for Exchange of Prisoners.
General S. A. MEREDITH.

FORT MONROE, VIRGINIA,
October 8, 1863.

SIR: I have the honor to acknowledge the receipt of your letter of October 5, 1863, and in reply I will state, that at my interview with the rebel agent of exchange I demanded the release of Colonel Streight and his command to aid to make up the equivalent for paroled officers and men declared exchanged by him. Mr. Ould declined, on the ground that on the last notice of exchange which we published, the balance was in his favor, at the same time handing me a written statement to that effect, which I had the honor to hand you in person. His reply was the same in relation to Colonel Powell.

Mr. Ould informed me that he should proceed to declare exchanges, whenever he conscientiously felt that he had the right to do so, for the purpose of putting men into the field.

I am, general, very respectfully, your obedient servant,
S. A. MEREDITH,
Brigadier General and Commissioner for Exchange.
Major General E. A. HITCHCOCK,
Commissioner of Exchanges, Washington, D. C.

OFFICE OF COMMISSIONER FOR EXCHANGE,
Fortress Monroe, Virginia, October 8, 1863.

SIR: In accordance with the instructions contained in your letter of the 5th instant, I submitted the letters from S. D. Culbertson and A. McInnes, esqs., therein enclosed, to Mr. Ould, informing him that we knew of no prisoners in our hands held under similar circumstances, and inviting him, if he knew of any, to name them, and make a mutual exchange. I explained to Mr. Ould that the United States authorities did not hold any person a prisoner on the ground that he was a citizen of the south, but always for some special cause. I also informed him that if he could not name any, that within twenty-four hours after any given time the United States authorities could seize any required number of secessionists in the south, to be exchanged for those referred to. Mr. Ould, in reply, stated that, notwithstanding, he would not make any special exchange, but that he was willing to make any arrangement which will be at all reciprocal, and he expresses himself perfectly willing to join in any *general* principle of exchange.

In this connexion I will state that Mr. Ould informed me that the object of the rebel authorities in arresting citizens was a retaliatory measure, and for the purpose of bringing to bear such a pressure on the United States authorities as to cause them to refrain from making more arrests of sympathizers with the south.

I am, general, very respectfully, your obedient servant,
S. A. MEREDITH,
Brigadier General and Commissioner for Exchange.
Major General E. A. HITCHCOCK,
Commissioner of Exchanges, Washington, D. C.

[Exchange Notice, No. 7.]

RICHMOND, *October* 16, 1863.

The following confederate officers and men are hereby declared duly exchanged:

1. All officers and men captured and paroled at any time previous to the first of September, 1863. This section, however, is not intended to include any officers or men captured at Vicksburg, July 4, 1863, except such as were declared exchanged by exchange notice No. 6, September 12, 1863, or are specifically named in this notice; but it does embrace all deliveries made at City Point, or other place, before September 1, 1863, and, with the limitation above named, all captures at Port Hudson, or any other place where the parties were released on parole.

2. The staff of Generals Pemberton, Stevenson, Bowen, Moore, Barton, S. D. Lee, Cummings, Harris, and Baldwin, and of Colonels Reynolds, Cockrell, and Dockery, the officers and men belonging to the engineer corps and sappers and miners, and the fourth and forty-sixth Mississippi regiments, all captured at Vicksburg, July 4, 1863.

3. The general officers captured at Vicksburg, July 4, 1863, were declared exchanged July 13, 1863.

ROBERT OULD,
Agent of Exchange.

HEADQUARTERS DEPARTMENT OF VIRGINIA,
Fort Monroe, October 17, 1863.

SIR: On the 22d day of May, 1863, Lieutenant Colonel Ludlow, the agent of exchange for the United States, enclosed you copies of General Orders No. 49 and No. 100, of War Department, announcing regulations and instructions for the government of United States forces in the field, in the matter of paroles, stating that these orders and the cartel are to govern our forces. When the cartel conflicts with the orders, they must be set aside. The cartel requires that prisoners of war shall be delivered at certain named places, and if they are not so delivered, the paroles cannot be valid. In consequence of the usage which has governed both parties up to that time, instructions were subsequently issued that paroles given before the 22d of May should be considered valid, though deliveries had not been made, as required by the cartel. In order to the putting in force these instructions it was not necessary to ask your consent; we were only bound to notify you that from that time the cartel would be rigidly adhered to by us, and the same course would be exacted of the confederate authorities. If you wish paroles recognized when the parties were not delivered at the places named in the cartel, you "ask that paroles not in conformity with the stipulations of the cartel should be regarded as valid."

I will now proceed to show that your declaration of September 12 was not in accordance with the cartel. Your reference to acts of Lieutenant Colonel Ludlow does not sustain you, for, according to your own letter, Lieutenant Colonel Ludlow was declaring an exchange to cover a "balance due" on declarations previously made by you. The troops thus declared exchanged by Lieutenant Colonel Ludlow are as follows:

51st regiment of Indiana volunteers	371
75th regiment of Indiana volunteers	268
3d regiment of Ohio volunteers	311
Tennessee cavalry	58
	1,008
Paroled at Mount Sterling	463
	1,471

You state that the "excess," without taking into account the Mount Sterling captures, was 2,290, whereas the whole number, including said captures, amount only to 1,471.

If in making up this balance Lieutenant Colonel Ludlow failed to give rolls and numbers, it does not justify you in anticipating a declaration by me, without furnishing me either rolls or numbers, or giving me time to consult the records to make them up for myself. When the paroling is properly done both parties have rolls, and then there can be little difficulty in arranging an exchange to be simultaneously declared.

You state that when the federal troops were declared exchanged to the 6th of May, the confederates were declared exchanged to the 23d of May, inclusive. I have nothing to show that the exchanges on both sides were not alike. The confederate prisoners delivered between the two dates amount to 5,083 privates, and if we have already received equivalents for them they should be deducted from my former computation. Without counting these, the number covered by your declaration of September 12, and the subsequent explanatory declaration of September 26, amounts to 29,450. The number of federal troops on parole to September 1, and declared exchanged, amounts to 23,911. The officers included are those paroled at Gettysburg and elsewhere; not those delivered at City Point. These numbers differ from those given to you before, because, in making up that calculation, all enlisted men were counted alike, whereas non-commissioned officers should have been counted as two privates.

Giving you the credit for the 5,083 enlisted men which you state were delivered at City Point between the 6th and the 23d of May, and declared exchanged by Colonel Ludlow, you are now in our debt 5,539 enlisted men.

You state that you have in your possession valid paroles amounting to 16,000 men. For all the prisoners that we claim as on parole we can show the rolls of delivery at the places named in the cartel, receipted by confederate officers; and if you can show similar rolls of the 16,000 men you speak of, they will of course be recognized as valid, and you will be credited with them.

Respectfully, your obedient servant,
S. A. MEREDITH,
Brigadier General and Commissioner for Exchange.
Hon. ROBERT OULD,
Agent of Exchange, Richmond, Virginia.

RICHMOND, *October* 20, 1863.

SIR: More than a month ago I asked your acquiescence to a proposition that all officers and soldiers on both sides should be released in conformity with the provisions of the cartel. In order to obviate the difficulties between us, I suggested that all officers and men on both sides should be released, unless they were subject to charges, in which event, the opposite government should have the right of retaining one or more hostages if the retention was not justified. "You stated to me in conversation that this proposition was very fair," (this statement is not true,) and that you would ask the consent of your government to it. As usual, you have as yet made no response. I tell you frankly I do not expect any. Perhaps you may disappoint me, and tell me that you reject or accept the proposition. I write this letter for the purpose of bringing to your recollection my proposition, and of dissipating the idea that seems to have been purposely encouraged by your public papers, that the confederate government has refused or objected to a system of exchanges.

In order to avoid any mistake in that direction, I now propose that all officers and men on both sides be released in conformity with the provisions of the cartel, the excess on one side or the other to be on parole. Will you accept this? I have no expectation of an answer, but, perhaps, you may give one. If it does come, I hope it will be soon.

Respectfully, your obedient servant,
ROBERT OULD,
Agent of Exchange.
Brig. Gen. S. A. MEREDITH,
Agent of Exchange.

CONFEDERATE STATES OF AMERICA,
War Department, Richmond, Va., October 27, 1863.

SIR: In reply to your communication of the 17th instant, I state that General Orders Nos. 49 and 100 were not sent to me at the same time. I received General Order No. 49 long before No. 100 was delivered to me. Their respective dates will show that to be the fact. My own personal recollection is, that General Order No. 100 was never communicated in a letter. It is my habit faithfully to keep all letters written by the federal agent of exchange. A careful search of the records of my office does not disclose any letter from Lieutenant

Colonel Ludlow communicating General Order No. 100. Lieutenant Colonel Ludlow met me at City Point on the 23d of May, 1863, and he then and there delivered to me General Order No. 100, stating that the principles therein announced would, in the future, control the operations of the forces of the United States. No written communication accompanied it. If any one was ever written to accompany it, I never received it. You are in error, therefore, when you say that Lieutenant Colonel Ludlow on the 22d May, 1863, enclosed copies of General Orders No. 49 and No. 100, announcing regulations and instructions for the government of the United States forces in the field in the matter of paroles, stating that these orders and the cartel were to govern your forces, and that when the cartel conflicted with the orders they were to be set aside. Independent of the facts of the case, I am justified in saying that any such communication would have been very extraordinary. It would not only have admitted that the general orders were in violation of the cartel, but would have declared that the later general order which, on its face, was announced to be the controlling law, should be set aside by the provisions contained in an earlier paper.

I again assert that the only notification I ever received as to your successive changes of purpose in the matter of paroles was from your own general orders, according to their respective dates, delivered to me without any further comment than I have already communicated to you.

You further say my "reference to the acts of Lieutenant Colonel Ludlow" does not sustain me. You further say the troops thus declared exchanged by Lieutenant Colonel Ludlow are as follows :

51st regiment Indiana volunteers	371
75th regiment Indiana volunteers	268
3d regiment Ohio volunteers	311
Tennessee cavalry	58
	1,008
Paroled at Mount Sterling	463
	1,471

Permit me to say that I read this paragraph of your letter with very great surprise. In my letter of the 2d instant, which you were contesting, I gave at length the communications of Lieutenant Colonel Ludlow, and by reference to it you will find that not only are the regiments which you have named therein mentioned, but also the Holly Springs capture, numbering 1,383 privates ; the 91st Illinois regiment, numbering 649 privates ; the officers and men of the Indianola, numbering 69 privates ; and the 80th regiment Illinois volunteers, numbering 400 privates. Not only is that the case, but your enumeration of 1,471 privates in the specified regiments is incorrect. The true aggregate is 1,676 privates. You misname one of the regiments also. The regiment declared exchanged was not the 75th Indiana, but the 73d.

In an interview with me at City Point, in the presence of Major Mulford, you admitted that all confederate officers and soldiers delivered at City Point before the 23d of May, 1863, were declared exchanged, while the federal soldiers were only declared exchanged up to May 6, 1863. Yet in your letter written subsequent to this admission you say you "have nothing to show that exchanges on both sides were not alike." Since your letter of the 17th, on our last interview, you made the same admission. If the fact is denied at any time, I stand prepared to prove it.

As to your computation, based upon my declarations of exchange, I refer you to my letter of the 2d of October, 1863. Every statement therein contained is strictly and accurately correct. I again assert, what I am ready to prove, that

I have in my possession more valid paroles of your officers and men than would be an equivalent for the exchanges I have declared up to this date.

Respectfully, your obedient servant,

ROBERT OULD,
Agent of Exchange.

Brig. Gen. S. A. MEREDITH,
Agent of Exchange.

CONFEDERATE STATES OF AMERICA,
War Department, Richmond, Virginia, October 27, 1863.

SIR: I enclose to you a memorandum of the paroles to which I have referred in several recent communications. Most of these paroles, you will observe, are antecedent to May 23, 1863. The reason why these paroles have not been heretofore discharged is, that up to July, 1863, we had the advantage of prisoners and paroles. Not one of these paroles is covered by any declaration of exchange, except the one lately made by you. For no one of them have I received any equivalent. All of them, since the date of your General Order No. 207, were given in pursuance of a distinct agreement between the commanders of two opposing armies. I have many other paroles in my possession, but I have only presented those which are within the terms of your general orders, according to their respective dates.

I understand there are other paroles coming within the same general orders, which were given by your officers and men on the other side of the Mississippi river. They as yet have not reached me. When they do, and when I show they are within the scope of your general orders, I will claim them; otherwise, I will discard them.

I have also received other informal paroles, which I have sent back for correction. These were also within the provisions of your general orders. When they are returned, I will claim them also.

Respectfully, your obedient servant,

ROBERT OULD,
Agent of Exchange.

Brig. Gen. S. A. MEREDITH,
Agent of Exchange.

Tabular statement of the number of valid federal paroles.

[This paper was sent by Mr. Ould to General Meredith, with a letter dated October 27, 1863.]

Where captured.	By whom.	When.	No. of prisoners.
Lavergne, Tennessee	General Wheeler	December 11 and 31, 1862	128
Lexington, Tennessee	General Forest	December 17, 1862	140
Benton Station, Tennessee	do	December 18 and 22, 1862	45
Near Spring creek, Tennessee	do	December 19, 1862	110
Trenton, Tennessee	do	December 20, 1862	694
Near Rutherford Station, Tenn.	do	December 21, 1862	144
Union City	do	December 23, 1862	86
Parker's Cross Roads & Dresden	do	Dec. 25, 1862, and Jan. 9, 1863	268
Kentucky and Tennessee	General Morgan	Dec. 7, 1862, and Jan. 27, 1863	190
Tennessee	General Wheeler	Dec. 30, 1862, and Jan. 5, 1863	381
Liberty, Tennessee	General Morgan	Dec. 26, 1862, and Feb. 13, 1863	78
Kentucky and Tennessee	do	Dec. 20, 1862, and Jan. 10, 1863	2,025
Near Murfreesboro', Tennessee	General Bragg	December 31, 1862	559
Galveston and Houston, Texas	Receipted for at Baton Rouge	January 1 and 22, 1863	359
Tennessee	General Wheeler	January 10 and 14, 1863	318
Kentucky and Tennessee	Generals Wheeler & Morgan	Jan. 10 and Feb. 14, 1863	111
Steam-ram Queen of the West	Receipted for at Baton Rouge	February 14, 1863	21
Near Memphis, Tennessee	Jackson's cavalry	do	10
West Liberty and McMinnville	General Morgan	Feb. 14 and March 7, 1863	51
Spring Hill, Tennessee	Bragg's command	March 7, 1863	103
Liberty, Tennessee	do	do	134
Near Rappahannock, Virginia	Major Mosby	do	39
Bourbon county, Kentucky	General Marshall	April 11, 1863	3
Western Virginia	General Jones	do	375
Chancellorsville, Virginia	General Lee	May 1 and 4, 1863	1,709
Western Virginia	General Imboden	May and June, 1863	18
Banks's Ford, Virginia	General Lee	May 4, 1863	129
Fredericksburg, Virginia		do	126
Vicksburg and vicinity	Pemberton's command	do	492
Near Monticello, Tennessee	General Pegram	May 25, 1863	19
Hinds county, Mississippi	Captain Reiley, 8th Kentucky	May 26 and June 6, 1863	742
Eastern Virginia	Major Mosby	June 11	16
Rome, Georgia	Bragg's command	April 30 and May 2, 1863	66
Mississippi	do	May 12 and 22, 1863	17
Kentucky and Tennessee	do	May 1 and 20, 1863	85
Holly Springs, Mississippi	General Van Dorn	December, 1862	1,694
Baton Rouge, Louisiana		February 24, 1863	303
Paroled at Salisbury, N. C		May 24, 1863	1,394
Perrysville, Va., & Gettysburg, Pa.	General Lee	July 2, 1863	2,629
Dover, Pennsylvania	General Stewart	do	210
Rockville, Maryland	do	do	157
Paroled at Williamsport	do	July 13, 1863	75
Morris Island, South Carolina	General Beauregard	July, 1863	142
Near Chattanooga, Tennessee	General Bragg	September, 1863	2,372
Miscellaneous paroles			33
Total			18,867

OFFICE OF COMMISSIONER FOR EXCHANGE,
Fort Monroe, Virginia, October 29, 1863.

SIR: I am in receipt of your communication of the 20th instant, the tenor of which induces me to make some explanatory statements of facts with which it would seem you need to be reminded.

The system of exchanges of prisoners of war, determined in the existing cartel, was first interrupted by the declared purpose of the confederate government to make certain distinctions in the treatment of a particular class of troops, officers and men, in violation of the provisions of the cartel. This seems to have been the first step towards the irregularities which have culminated in your unequivocal declaration, reported by me to my government on the 18th instant, that "(you) will proceed to declare exchanges whenever (you) conscientiously feel that (you) have the right to do so, for the purpose of putting men into the field."

There can be no objection to your acting conscientiously in any given case, so long as your conscience is enlightened and guided by those laws of war which require obedience between belligerents to solemn agreements entered into by authorized commissioners, acting in the name of their respective superiors. But if you mean by the expression, your "conscientious sense of right," to substitute this sense of right for the requirements of an existing cartel, I can by no means concede to you that right; and if you do not mean this, I cannot understand what you mean by so vague and general a declaration. Judging by your recent proceedings, it seems that you have declared exchanged all confederate officers and soldiers on parole within what you claim as your lines, up to a very recent date, without having any proper right to do so, either under the cartel or under the laws of war.

The history of this matter, as I understand it, is briefly this: While my predecessor on duty at this place was here in discharge of the duties now committed to me, you at one time made a declaration of exchange, embracing no great number of prisoners of war, not in accordance with the requirements of the cartel, and you invited Colonel Ludlow, my predecessor, to make a corresponding declaration of equivalents. Such a declaration was made by Colonel Ludlow, doubtless without anticipating the magnitude of the evil which appears now as the result of that departure from the cartel, first inaugurated by yourself. Subsequently to my coming on duty here the events of the war threw upon your hands a large body of paroled officers and men, over 30,000, captured by General Grant at Vicksburg; and not long afterwards, some six thousand or more captured by General Banks at Port Hudson.

Suddenly, and without any proper conference or understanding with me, and but a few days prior to the important events at Chickamauga, as if for the express purpose of increasing the force of General Bragg against General Rosecrans, you gave me notice that, on the next day after the date of that notice, you would declare exchanged a large portion of the troops which had been captured by General Grant. When your declaration was made, it covered an indeterminate number of troops, designated by commands, brigades, divisions and corps, no definite number of either officers or men being designated. Up to that time you had delivered at City Point a certain number of prisoners of war for which you had receipts, by which you must have known the number you might claim the right to discharge from their parole. You did not think proper to limit yourself to this number, nor in any proper manner did you refer to it, but made your declaration of exchange in such indefinite terms as made it next to certain that you did not intend to be governed by the cartel.

On referring to the data furnished by the reports of General Grant, and now in the hands of the commissary general of prisoners at Washington, it was ascertained that you had discharged from parole by your declaration a very considerable number of your men, over and above any claim you might pretend to, founded on receipts for prisoners of war delivered from the south according to the cartel. Without referring to fractions, it appeared, from the best data in our hands, that you had discharged *three* for *two*, or one-third more than you were entitled to. You suggested that I should make a corresponding declaration of exchange, when, as I suppose you must have known, you had not delivered to me, nor had you valid paroles of our men, sufficient to cover the number declared exchanged by yourself; and when I proceeded to make the declaration extending to those men you had delivered, and stated to you my objections to your proceedings, you insisted that you had valid paroles for more than the number that you had declared exchanged, though you failed to produce those paroles or to give any account or history of them; and you then proceed to make a further declaration of exchange, ignoring the cartel altogether, basing your action upon no data communicated to me, the whole proceeding resting, as I suppose you will say, upon *your* sense of right, as if you were the only party having a *right* to an opinion on the subject; acting evidently in anticipation of the formal declaration, referred to at the commencement of this communication, that you will proceed to make declarations of exchange for the purpose of putting troops into the field whenever you think proper; and having now exhausted by a declaration of exchange the paroled prisoners in your hands, you propose to me the delivery of prisoners of war in our hands for whom you have no equivalents, or comparatively but very few, in order, as it were, that you may obtain possession of many thousands more men of your own, delivered or on parole, for the purpose of declaring them also exchanged, and putting them into the field, not in conformity with the existing cartel, nor in accordance with the usages of war, but whenever, in your individual judgment, you may think it proper to do so.

I have only to add that an easy inference from this statement is the answer I have to make to your proposal of the 20th instant, which is not accepted.

Respectfully, your obedient servant,

S. A. MEREDITH,
Brigadier General and Commissioner of Exchange.

Hon. ROBERT OULD,
Agent of Exchange.

WASHINGTON CITY, D. C., *October* 30, 1863.

SIR: I observe that Mr. Ould claims that if the paroles given at Gettysburg by our troops are not to be considered valid, the troops should be returned as captured, because an order requires our commanders to return troops when improperly paroled on the field of battle.

This pretension is so manifestly inadmissible, that I have not thought necessary to answer it in form.

The principles involved are these: paroles on the field of battle, often given in haste by an enemy unable to take care of or secure them, are informal and invalid *by the laws of war.*

As a measure of discipline in the army, an order was issued (the order appealed to by Mr. Ould) requiring officers not to receive, but to return prisoners when thus improperly paroled. This order is purely disciplinary in our service, and has nothing to do with the principle, *the law of war*, by which paroles improperly given are declared to be invalid. It might be considered as designed to give effect to the law of paroles, but in no sense would the conduct of our commanders under this order make valid paroles improperly given. A commander who should disobey this order might be tried for such disobedience, being answerable to the authority by which the order was given, but the requirements of the laws of war on the subject of paroles would be in no manner affected thereby.

Besides, the order to our commanders, referred to, was designed to take effect on the field of battle, or immediately thereafter, on the assumption that prisoners so returned upon the enemy would be left on the field, the enemy being supposed to be in no condition to secure them—the very reason why the law of war makes paroles thus given invalid. But this view is fully justified by the practice of the enemy. In a recent case a party, including Lieutenant Colonel Allston, (recently exchanged,) was informally paroled. The enemy immediately so declared, and ordered every officer and man upon duty. Lieutenant Colonel Allston, however, chose to act individually; and on the ground of having given his parole, he declared that he would not go upon duty until exchanged; and upon this view he delivered himself up to General Burnside, and then, but not until then, he became a prisoner of war. General Burnside considered his case peculiar, as manifesting a high sense of honor, and recommended his immediate exchange, which was accordingly ordered by the Secretary of War.

We do not deny the right to order that party on duty under the circumstances, precisely answering to the case of our own men at Gettysburg.

We do not claim that Lieutenant Colonel Allston was our prisoner under the parole he gave, but because he subsequently delivered himself into the hands of General Burnside.

With these views we claim that the Gettysburg paroles were invalid, and this principle must be adhered to.

Very respectfully, your obedient servant,
E. A. HITCHCOCK,
Major General Volunteers, &c.

Brigadier General S. A. MEREDITH,
Commissioner for Exchange of Prisoners.

CONFEDERATE STATES OF AMERICA,
War Department, Richmond, Virginia, October 31, 1863.

SIR: In relation to your communication of the 23d instant, enclosing a letter from W. P. Wood to General Hitchcock, I submit the following:

More than a year ago, recognizing the injustice of the arrest of non-combatants, I submitted the following proposition to the federal authorities, to wit: "that peaceable non-combatant citizens of both the United and Confederate States, who are not connected with any military organization, shall not be arrested by either the United States or confederate armies within the territory of the adverse party. If this proposition is too broad, let the only exception be the case of a temporary arrest of parties within army lines, where the arresting party has good reason to believe that their presence is dangerous to the safety of the army from the opportunity afforded of giving intelligence to the enemy. It is to be understood, however, in the latter case, the arrest is to cease as soon as the reason for making it ceases, in the withdrawal of the army, or for any other cause. This proposal is understood to include such arrests and imprisonments as are already in force."

Although this proposition, so reasonable and humane in its terms, has been before your government for more than a year, it has never been accepted. I now again call your attention to it. If it does not suit you, I will thank you to suggest any modification. I am willing to adopt any fair and reciprocal rule that will settle this matter on principle. It must, however, be settled by rule. It cannot with any safety be determined by "special cases."

You ask me if I will release your citizens against whom there are no charges. Would it not be more liberal to make that offer on your part as far as our citizens are concerned, before you ask our consent? You have kept confederate citizens in prison for many months without charges. Most of them have never had any charges preferred against them, although, in the opinion of your authorities, there were "special reasons" for their arrest. How easy is it to give or invent a special reason? In all probability there never has been an arrest and imprisonment on either side since this war began, for which there was not "a special cause." An arrest for retaliatory reasons, even, is special.

As far as the arrest of citizens of the Confederate States by our authorities is concerned, we will submit to no interference in any way by the federal government. It is matter with which you have nothing to do. The confederate authorities do not interfere with your arrests of your own people, no matter what injustice has been done to them. Any attempt on the part of the federal government to interpose in cases which only concern our authorities and the people of these Confederate States may be justly styled impertinent and meddlesome. As far, however, as the arrests of citizens of the adverse party is concerned, we are at all times ready to adopt any fair and reciprocal rule.

Respectfully, your obedient servant,

ROBERT OULD,
Agent of Exchange.

Brigadier General MEREDITH,
Agent of Exchange.

OFFICE OF EXCHANGE OF PRISONERS,
Richmond, Virginia, October 31, 1863.

SIR: Your communication of the 29th instant has been received, and its extraordinary and groundless statements read with surprise.

You first represent me as having informed you that I would proceed to declare exchanges whenever I conscientiously felt that I had the right to do so, for the purpose of putting men into the field. In another part of your letter I am charged with having stated that I would proceed to make declarations of exchange for the purpose of putting troops into the field whenever I thought proper. Both of these paragraphs are between quotation marks, to indicate that I had communicated them. Moreover, they are mentioned as being my "unequivocal declaration." Upon a faithful examination of my correspondence with you and your predecessor, I can find no instance in which such language has been used by me. Will you inform me of the date of any such communication, or furnish me with a copy of it? If you cannot, you will certainly deem me justified in denouncing your statement as utterly without foundation in truth.

Upon these premises you have proceeded to throw off sundry sentences more flippant than worthy of notice. As usual, however, you finish the paragraph which contains them with a misstatement in asserting that I "have declared exchanged all confederate officers and soldiers on parole" within our lines, "up to a very recent date." I have done no such thing. I specially excepted the larger part of the Vicksburg capture.

You then proceed to give what you call "a history of this matter." That history, like many others, turns out to be a romance. Lieutenant Colonel Ludlow's declarations of exchange, to which I referred in my letter of October 2, 1863, were not made in response to any invitation from me, or in consequence of any previous declarations which I had made. I did not "inaugurate" what you term "a departure from the cartel." The correspondence of the office very clearly shows that fact.

You are wrong also in your statement that the Vicksburg capture was subsequent to your "coming to duty" at Fortress Monroe. I received official communications from Lieutenant Colonel Ludlow as late as July 22, 1863—weeks after the Vicksburg surrender—and none from you until the 25th of the same month.

You charge that the declaration of exchange bearing date September 12, 1863, was made "as if for the express purpose of increasing the force of General Bragg against General Rosecrans." This is also untrue. The declaration was not published until several days after the 12th, although it bore that date. Not one of the officers or men named in that declaration of exchange was on the battle-field of Chickamauga.

You further say I must have known that I had not delivered to you, nor had I valid paroles of your men, sufficient to cover the number declared exchanged by me. I knew exactly the contrary, and so informed you. On the 11th of September, 1863, in announcing the declaration of exchange I would make on the following day, I wrote to you that I had "in my possession more valid paroles of your officers and men than would be an equivalent for the officers and men" enumerated in the exchange notice. I have made the same statement to you more than once since. I am prepared to prove that it was true each time it was uttered.

You say *your* declaration of exchange extended to those whom I had *delivered.* If you mean that it was limited to such you are incorrect, for it declared exchanged all officers and men of the United States army captured and paroled at any time previous to the 1st of September, 1863, and included many thousands of prisoners taken and paroled by our cavalry and other forces in numerous States of the confederacy, never delivered by me. I have already furnished you a memorandum of at least sixteen thousand of these paroled prisoners.

You say I failed to produce the paroles, or to give any account or history of them. If you mean that I refused to do so, it is not true. I offered to produce them at any time, and importuned you to agree to some principle by which they could be computed and adjusted. When I last met you at City Point you requested me for the first time to send to you a memorandum of the paroles claimed as valid by me. I furnished you with the list on the 27th instant, that being the first day after your request on which a flag of truce boat appeared at City Point.

You say I then proceeded to make a further declaration of exchange, "ignoring the cartel altogether," and resting the whole proceeding, as you suppose, on my "sense of right." There again you are mistaken. I did not rest the proceeding entirely upon my sense of right. I relied, in some measure, upon yours, and to that extent its propriety may be doubtful. In communicating to you exchange notice No. 7, which is the one to which you refer, I wrote to you as follows: "I herewith enclose to you a declaration of exchange, which I shall publish in a day or two. You will perceive it is based upon the declaration of exchange communicated to me in your letter of the 24th of September last. In my notice I have followed your phraseology. I would have preferred another form of declaration, more in accordance with the circumstances of the case. Inasmuch, however, as my declaration to a considerable extent is retaliatory of yours, I have deemed it more appropriate to follow your own form of expression." Your letter of the 24th of September declared that "all officers and men of the United States army captured and paroled at any time previous to the 1st of September, 1863, are duly exchanged." On the 16th of October following I declared exchanged "all (confederate) officers and men captured and paroled at any time previous to the 1st of September, 1863." If that was "ignoring the cartel," as you charge, I only followed your example. Our declarations of exchange were precisely similar, except that in another part of my notice I reserved from its operation the larger part of the Vicksburg paroles. If I had followed your "sense of right," as I then had, and still claim, the right to do, I would have included all.

The confederate authorities take it unto themselves as a proud and honorable boast that they have determined all these matters of paroles and exchanges according to their "sense of right," and not by any views of temporary expediency. In following that guide, they have at least shunned some examples furnished by your government. They have never, in violation of their general orders, and without notice to the adverse party, ordered their paroled officers and men to break their solemn covenant, and, without exchange, lift their arms against their captors. They have, therefore, escaped the pangs of that retributive justice which made your general order of July 3, 1863, though so well suited to the meridian of Gettysburg, invalidate the paroles given at Port Hudson on the 9th of the same month. Upon further reflection, I am sure you will be satisfied that it does not become your authorities, who have chosen, whenever they felt so disposed, without notice, or consent from us, to repudiate the established usages of exchange and put new constructions upon the cartel, to complain that others have acted according to their sense of right.

Not content with all the misstatements of fact which I have cited, you have, in your letter of the 29th instant, descended to a malignant and wanton aspersion of the motives of the confederate authorities in making the proposal contained in my letter of the 20th instant. You were asked to agree "that all officers and men on both sides should be released, the excess on one side or the other to be on parole." It would have been injustice enough to the many thousands of your prisoners in our hands, and to those of ours in your custody, simply to have declined the proposal. But you have thought proper to add to your refusal the gratuitous insult to the Confederate States of intimating that their fair and honest offer was made for the purpose of putting into the field officers and men fraudulently exchanged. This calumny is as destitute of foundation in fact as it is despicable in spirit.

In conclusion, let me tell you that the purpose of your letter is apparent. It has been well known for a long time that your authorities are opposed to a fair and regular exchange of prisoners under the cartel. In rejecting my proposition you have endeavored to conceal under a cloud of vague charges and unfounded statements, the determination at which your government long since arrived. Why not be frank once? Why not say, without any further subterfuges, that you have reached the conclusion that our officers and soldiers are more valuable, man for man, than yours?

Respectfully, your obedient servant,

ROBERT OULD,
Agent of Exchange.

Brigadier General S. A. MEREDITH,
Agent of Exchange.

WASHINGTON CITY, D. C., *November 6, 1863.*

SIR: Your communication of the 29th ultimo has been received, forwarding what purports to be a tabular statement of the number of valid paroles claimed by Mr. Ould, with a copy of his letter, accompanying it, to yourself, of the 27th ultimo.

This tabular statement covers a claim to 18,867 paroles of federal troops, without distinction of grade; no officers or non-commissioned officers being noticed as among the prisoners. The statement professes to enumerate forty-four places where captures were made, with the names of captors, and dates of capture; the number said to have been captured being carried out in figures.

This statement may include some prisoners captured and paroled according to the laws of war; but, if so, it is impossible to distinguish them by any evidence in the statement itself. A few are said to have been "receipted for" at Baton Rouge, January 22, 1863, and February 14, 1863, which may be verified; and some evidence may come to light confirming the alleged captures by Generals Lee, Bragg, and possibly some others; but, on the whole, the statement is unsatisfactory, and in its present form is regarded as without credit and not entitled to consideration.

The statement does not show in any one instance by whom the prisoners were received, or to whom or even where they were delivered, leaving it to be presumed that they were for the most part paroled on the instant of capture, without authority under the cartel, in not being "reduced to actual possession," contrary to both the laws of war as set forth in Order No. 100 of 1863, and the provisions of the cartel. Order No. 100 merely publishes the laws of war, and the cartel is entirely in harmony with it.

The orders on this subject subsequently issued, and to which Mr. Ould appeals, were expressly designed to give effect to those laws, and to the cartel, and were in no manner intended to abrogate, and neither do they abrogate or modify, the one or the other. If the enemy wishes in good faith to carry out the orders he refers to, the proper course would be to issue similar orders, and for a like purpose; in which case, there might be some hope of a compliance with both the cartel and the laws of war.

Mr. Ould's effort to have recognized certain paroles as valid, which have been informally and improperly made, embracing, so far as we can know from his statements, many *citizens* in Kentucky, Tennessee, and elswhere, (no particular place being named in some instances,) by appealing to northern orders, is a mere perversion of the clear and manifest design of those orders; that design being, as already stated, to enforce, and not to nullify, the laws of war. We appeal to those orders, and intend to be governed by them, and if the enemy would assume them, and be governed by them also, all difficulties on the subject of paroles would cease. By Mr. Ould's mode of application or misapplication of those orders, he would use them to destroy and not to enforce the laws of war.

The laws of war are first in order, imposing obligations upon belligerents; and they continue to be obligatory upon both parties, unless modified by a special agreement under a cartel, which, when agreed upon, becomes the highest authority in all specified cases included in the cartel, leaving the laws of war in full operation in all cases not provided for in the cartel; a cartel being analogous to a treaty of commerce between nations, which may modify the natural laws of trade or commerce, binding both parties to the treaty.

The orders of a general in the field, or of a general-in-chief of one of the belligerents, are only operative within the field of the general's command, and can have no effect to modify either the laws of war or the provisions of a particular cartel. Such orders are purely disciplinary in the army where issued, and can neither bind an enemy, nor can an enemy appeal to them to justify his departure from or violation of either a particular cartel, or the laws of war. A departure from such an order within the army subject to the authority issuing the order might subject the offender to punishment within his own army, but could not be appealed to, to make a parole valid, which, by the laws of war, or by the provisions of a particular cartel, would be disowned as not valid.

While we set forth these principles as binding, we deny emphatically that the orders appealed to by Mr. Ould sanction his departure from the laws of war or the cartel, the express purpose of Order No. 207 (1863) being to enforce the provisions of the existing cartel. It sets out by an appeal, in paragraph I, to the cartel, by its date and the date of the order by which it was published, the provisions of which are to be enforced; and this is again set forward in paragraph II.

Order No. 207 publishes a very important law of war, in paragraph IV, in announcing that "the obligations imposed by the general laws and usages of war, upon the non-combatant inhabitants of a section of country passed over by an invading army, cease when the military occupation ceases; and any pledge or parole given by such persons, in regard to future service, is null and of no effect." This paragraph of Order No. 207 does not originate, it merely announces, the law of war on the subject to which it refers; but it is particularly significant, in view of the probable character of many of the paroles claimed as valid, in the tabular statement furnished by Mr. Ould, in which, under the head of "where captured," the statement uses generalities which can in no sense be received. Thus, captures are said to have been made in "Kentucky and Tennessee;" in "Tennessee;" in "Kentucky and Tennessee," (again;) in "Tennessee," (again;) in "Kentucky and Tennessee," (a third time;) in "Barbour county, Kentucky," (whether soldiers or citizens we cannot tell;) in "Western Virginia;"

in "Western Virginia," (again;) in "Hinds county, Mississippi;" in "Eastern Virginia;" in "Mississippi;" in "Kentucky and Tennessee," (for the fourth time,) &c.

In fine, the statement is wholly informal and without authority.

You will please furnish Mr. Ould a certified copy of this communication.

Very respectfully, your obedient servant,

E. A. HITCHCOCK,
Major General Volunteers, Com'r for the Exchange of Prisoners.

Brigadier General S. A. MEREDITH,
Commissioner for the Exchange of Prisoners.

OFFICE OF COMMISSIONER FOR EXCHANGE,
Fort Monroe, Va., November 7, 1863.

SIR: In your communication of October 27 you state, "that General Orders Nos. 49 and 100 were not sent to you at the same time." I forward you herewith a copy of Lieutenant Colonel Ludlow's letter, enclosing to you the two orders mentioned, and bearing date May 22, 1863.

These two orders announced general rules based on the usages of war, which, in the absence of any specific agreement between belligerents, should govern in paroling prisoners of war; but in this case a cartel had already been agreed upon, and no order of either party could set aside any of its provisions. For instance, a commander, on being captured, might under some circumstances give a parole for himself and his command, without violating General Order No. 100, (which includes General Order No. 49;) but unless the paroling was done at City Point, or other named place, it would be in violation of the cartel, and the paroles must therefore be set aside as invalid. No exception could be taken to this course by the party granting the parole, because the validity of the parole depends on a strict compliance with the provisions of the cartel; and when any other course is followed than that pointed out by that instrument, any claim based upon it must fail. Paragraph 130 of Order 100, which prescribes the duties which a paroled soldier may perform, is also, to some extent, set aside by the cartel, which restricts these duties to a much more limited field than the order. Paragraph 131 is also made inoperative by the cartel, because it could only apply to paroles not given at the points designated for delivery; all such paroles are by the cartel made invalid, and the paroling party could therefore have no pretext for claiming their recognition. If such a claim could be admitted, the effect at Gettysburg would have been, to give to General Lee the privilege of placing his prisoners in our hands, to be delivered to him, at our own charge, at City Point, which is so manifestly absurd that even you cannot claim it. General Order No. 207 was intended simply to announce to the army that the irregular practice of paroling small squads of men and individuals, without rolls or other reliable evidence of any kind, which had very generally prevailed, must be discontinued, and that thereafter the cartel should be rigidly adhered to. This announcement had been made to the confederate authorities through you.

There have been no "successive changes of purpose in the matter of paroles," as you assert, nor changes of any kind, except so far as to return to a strict observance of the cartel; and this is a change, the propriety of which I do not think you can question.

The figures which I gave you in my letter of October 17 were not given as embracing all declared exchanged in General Order 167, of June 8, but only those which Lieutenant Colonel Ludlow used to make up the balance due him after arranging that declaration with you. It was the declaration which Lieutenant Colonel Ludlow made to cover this balance that you cite as the precedent which authorized you to announce so unexpectedly your declarations of September 12. The 80th Illinois, 311 men—not 400, as you say—was accidentally omitted from my letter, and, by a clerical error, 73d Indiana was written 75th Indiana. Paragraphs 5 and 6 of General Order 167 cover the troops referred to, and other paragraphs cover the captures mentioned by you. Any discrepancy in numbers declared exchanged at that time, on either side, is of little consequence, as up to the date of that order it is assumed that the exchange account was satisfactorily balanced.

Respectfully, your obedient servant,

S. A. MEREDITH,
Brigadier General and Commissioner for Exchange.

Hon. ROBERT OULD,
   Agent of Exchange, Richmond, Virginia.

OFFICE OF COMMISSIONER FOR EXCHANGE,
Fort Monroe, Virginia, November 12, 1863.

SIR : I acknowledge the receipt of your communication of October 31.

I would have been surprised at its contents had I not been previously acquainted with your habit of special pleading and of perverting the truth. In the last interview but one which I had with you, you stated to me distinctly and unequivocally that you would make declarations of exchange whenever you conscientiously felt that you had the right so to do, *for the purpose of putting men into the field.* You made this statement not only once, but two or three times. In my previous interviews with you, I had taken the precaution to have verbal propositions of any importance made by you reduced to writing. On this occasion I refrained from my usual course—now much to my regret, as I will do you the justice to say that I have no doubt you have forgotten what occurred at that meeting.

The following extracts from two of your letters will probably serve to convince you that it is highly probable that, while laboring under the excitement hinted at above, you may have made the statement attributed to you. From your letter dated October 2, 1863, I take the following :

" I now inform you, in view of the recent declaration of exchange made by you, coupled with your failure either to agree to or decline the proposition made to you on the 24th of August last, in relation to paroles, that the confederate authorities will consider themselves entirely at liberty to pursue any course as to exchanges of paroles which they may deem right and proper."

Again, in your letter to me of October 16, you stated as follows :

" I reserve to *myself* the right to make further declarations of exchange from time to time, based upon the paroles in my office, until I have declared exchanged a number of confederate soldiers equal to that of federal troops declared exchanged by your last notice."

In these two extracts you arrogate to your government and yourself the right to declare exchanges. Of course, a government in as prosperous a condition as the confederacy, with men in superabundance to put into the field, would not declare men exchanged for that purpose, nor would a high-toned, honorable gentleman, who has reserved to *himself* the right to declare exchanges, use that right with the idea of putting men in the field. Yet it is well known that many officers and men captured at Vicksburg were in the battle of Chickamauga. I deem it proper here to say a few words in relation to the 18,000 paroles which you state you have in your possession, and which you claim as valid. You rest the validity of these paroles (which I have never seen, and which you acknowledge to have been accumulating for many months) on general orders of the United States government, Nos. 49 and 100. These two orders announce general rules based on the usages of war; but a cartel having been agreed upon, no order of either party could set aside its provisions, which I have stated to you on several occasions. For instance, a commander on being captured might, under some circumstances, give a parole for himself and his command without violating General Order No. 100 (which includes General Order No. 49;) but unless the paroling was done at City Point or other named place, it would be in violation of the cartel. Nor could exceptions be taken to this course by the party granting the parole, because the validity of the parole depends on a strict compliance with the provisions of the cartel. Paragraph 130 of Order 100, which prescribes the duties that a paroled soldier may perform, is also to some extent set aside by the cartel, which restricts these duties to a much more limited field than the order. Paragraph 131, which you attempt to make so much of, is also rendered inoperative by the cartel, because it could only apply to paroles not given at the points designated for delivery; but all such paroles are by the cartel made invalid, and the paroling party, therefore, has no pretext for claiming their recognition. Had such a claim been admitted, the effect at Gettysburg would have been to give to General Lee the privilege of placing his prisoners in our hands, to be delivered to him at City Point at our own charge—a claim so manifestly absurd that I am surprised that even you should have had the assurance to make it. Yet, on precisely this ground rests the foundation for the 18,000 paroles which you claim as valid.

Paroles on the field of battle, often given in haste by an enemy unable to take care of or receive them, are informal and invalid by the *laws of war*. Most of the paroles above mentioned were taken by guerillas, bushwhackers, and detached commands in the west. No possession was ever had, no delivery was ever made, and no rolls have ever been furnished of those giving them. On the capture of a town by a cavalry raid, the command remained long enough to take the paroles of the unarmed citizens there, and then decamped, leaving the paroled men behind, and forwarding the paroles to accumulate in your office in Richmond; yet you have the assurance to say that you expect the United States government to exchange prisoners legitimately captured in battle, and now held in custody, for such paroles as these.

It is well for you to write letters filled with well-feigned indignation at any imputation upon the integrity or honesty of your government or yourself, for publication in the south, to delude the suffering people there into the belief that you and your government are doing everything to cause a resumption of exchanges; but I feel it my duty to say, that your principles are so flexible, and your rule of action so slightly influenced by a sense of truth, honesty, or honor, that I find it almost impossible to arrive at any fair understanding with you on the subject, and all my efforts thus far, for the above reason, have been fruitless.

In your communication of October 27 you use the following language: "I state that General Orders Nos. 49 and 100 were not sent to me at the same time. I received General Order No. 49 *long before* No. 100 was delivered to me. Their respective dates will show that to be the fact. My own personal recollection is that General Order No. 100 was never communicated in a letter." You then proceed to impress the public with an idea of your careful habits as follows: "It is my habit faithfully to keep all letters written by the federal agent of exchanges." But this most important letter happened to be mislaid! which intelligence you convey to the southern public as follows: "A careful search of the records of my office does not disclose any letter from Lieutenant Colonel Ludlow communicating General Order No. 100." On November 7th I sent you a copy of the letter hereto annexed, copied from Lieutenant Colonel Ludlow's letter-book; but through fear that it might have met the fate of the original and miscarried, I send it again:

"HEADQUARTERS DEPARTMENT OF VA., 7TH ARMY CORPS,
"*Fort Monroe, Virginia, May* 22, 1863.

"SIR: I have the honor to enclose to you copies of General Orders Nos. 49 and 100, of the War Department, announcing regulations and instructions for the government of the United States forces in the field in the matter of paroles. These, together with the stipulations of the cartel, will govern our army. I would invite your special attention to article 7 of the cartel, which provides that all prisoners of war shall be sent to places of delivery therein specified. The execution of this article will obviate much discussion and difficulty growing out of the mode, time, and place of giving paroles. No paroles or exchanges will be considered binding except those under the stipulations of said article, permitting commanders of two opposing armies to exchange or release on parole at other points mutually agreed on by said commanders.

"I am, very respectfully, your obedient servant,
"WILLIAM H. LUDLOW,
"*Lieut. Colonel and Agent for Exchange of Prisoners.*

"Hon. ROBERT OULD,
"*Agent for Exchange of Prisoners.*"

It appears to me that you have been unfortunate on two occasions: first, in forgetting the statement you made to me, alluded to in the beginning of this communication; and second, in your not having received the above letter. As communications between the agents of exchanges go through but two hands, (the assistant agents,) it strikes me as a little extraordinary that out of hundreds the above should be the only one to miscarry.

The denial of facts which abound in your last letter, though they may have some weight in the south, will not avail to convince the people of the north that you are not utterly reckless of integrity and fairness, and full of *finesse* in your declarations of exchanges, and the foundations you claim for them.

Respectfully,

S. A. MEREDITH,
Brigadier General and Commissioner for Exchanges.

Hon. ROBERT OULD,
Agent of Exchange, Richmond, Va.

CONFEDERATE STATES OF AMERICA,
War Department, Richmond, Virginia, November 21, 1863.

SIR: I have received the letter of General Hitchcock, relating to the memorandum of paroles, which I forwarded to you.

General Hitchcock seems to have misapprehended my purpose somewhat in sending you that memorandum. You requested a list of the paroles which I claimed, and the paper which I sent to you was only intended to be understood as a memorandum in the way of notice to you. I did not expect you to agree to recognize the paroles therein referred to in such a general way, upon the mere presentation of the paper. The evidence which supports that memorandum of paroles is on file in my office. If we could only have agreed upon the principle by which they should be computed and adjusted, all the rest would have been easy work. I would have presented the paroles themselves, or authenticated lists of them. The fact that they were given, the circumstances under which they were given, the parties giving them, would all appear upon the face of the papers in proper form. As General Hitchcock seems to indicate a willingness to reopen this matter, I will state for his benefit frankly the principles by which I propose to be governed.

1. I will not claim the paroles of citizens. All the paroles which I will produce will be those of federal soldiers in actual service at the time of capture.

2. I will show the particular locality where the parties were captured, the command to which they belonged, the command which captured them, and the precise date of each transaction.

3. I will accompany the presentation with such full and particular evidence as will enable you to verify the truth of the case by your own records and the statements of your own officers and soldiers.

4. More than thirty of the forty-four items in my memorandum are cases of captures made previous to the 22d of May, 1863. It has never at any time been alleged that I had any notice before that time that paroling upon the battle-field was not to be permitted. The federal authorities have charged against me paroles taken upon the battle-field up to that date, and have received credit for them. I would have received credit for these items many months ago, if you had have had paroles or prisoners of ours to have off-setted against them. I will thank General Hitchcock to inform me upon what principle he can reject those thirty-odd items. If he wants evidence that I have allowed precisely similar paroles, I will furnish it.

5. As to such of the paroles as were given between the 22d of May, 1863, and the 3d of July, (the date of General Order No. 207,) I shall contend that they shall be allowed under the provisions of paragraph 131 of General Order No. 100. I will allow any similar paroles given to you during the same period.

6. As to all paroles given after the 3d of July, 1863, I will allow General Order No. 207 to have full force. No paroles from and after that date are to be valid, unless the paroling is in pursuance of the agreement of the commanders of two opposing armies.

7. In my memorandum the officers and non-commissioned officers are reduced to *privates*. There are but very few, if any, commissioned officers on the lists. They have already been exchanged and checked off. This is of itself proof that your authorities have heretofore recognized these paroles. The lists and paroles will show the grade of all the parties.

8. I have been greatly misunderstood by General Hitchcock, if he thinks I have refused to be governed by your general orders. General Hitchcock says, "We appeal to those orders, and intend to be governed by them; and if the enemy would assume them, and be governed by them also, all difficulties on the subject of paroles would cease." I have already expressed my willingness to be governed by your general orders "on the subject of paroles." It was my original proposition. I adhere to it still. Let, then, "all difficulties cease."

9. If our present difficulties are to cease, let me, for the sake of future harmony, suggest that there be some definite meaning attached to the phrase "commanders of two opposing armies." Who are such commanders? We can readily understand that General Lee and General Meade are such. But is General Thomas the commander of one of the opposing armies at Chattanooga, or is it General Grant? Was General Pemberton the commander of an opposing army, when he was subject to the orders of General Johnston, who was in his immediate neighborhood? Was General Gardner the commander of an opposing army at Port Hudson? If so, is not every one who holds a separate command such a commander? Does size constitute an army? If a captain or lieutenant is on detached service, is he the commander of an opposing army, and can he be released on parole by an agreement made with the officer who captured him, if he is on detached service? I make these inquiries of General Hitchcock in no captious spirit. They do present difficulties to my mind, and I should like to know what is to be considered as the true interpretation of the phrase. All the captures after the 3d of July, 1863, which I ask you to recognize, were in pursuance of "an agreement between the commanders of two opposing armies." I cannot see how any difficulty can arise between General

Hitchcock and myself after his letter, except as to captures between May 22, 1863, and July 3, 1863. They are but very few in number.

I will thank you to send this letter, or a copy of it, to General Hitchcock.

Respectfully, your obedient servant,

ROBERT OULD,
Agent of Exchange.

Brigadier General S. A. MEREDITH,
Agent of Exchange.

OFFICE OF COMMISSIONER FOR EXCHANGE,
Fort Monroe, Virginia, November 25, 1863.

SIR: I have the honor to report to you that I have just returned from an interview with the rebel agent of exchange, Mr. Ould. In consequence of the reports of the terrible cruelties inflicted upon our prisoners in Richmond, which were given to me by the surgeons who were just released, I deemed it a fit opportunity to renew an offer to Mr. Ould, which, though unofficial, I stated to him would, no doubt, if accepted, be carried out by the United States authorities, and which I would urge them to do by every means in my power. The offer was this: To send immediately to City Point twelve thousand or more confederate prisoners, to be exchanged for the federal soldiers now confined in the south. This proposition was distinctly and unequivocally refused by Mr. Ould, on the ground that it would be making twelve thousand or more special exchanges. He stated that the only condition upon which he would agree to the release of our prisoners would be that we should send south a number of confederate prisoners equal to that of federal prisoners in their hands, and parole and send within their lines the balance of the confederates in the custody of the United States authorities.

Very respectfully, your obedient servant,

S. A. MEREDITH,
Brigadier General and Commissioner for Exchange.

Major General E. A. HITCHCOCK,
Commissioner of Exchanges, Washington, D. C.

WASHINGTON CITY, D. C., *November* 23, 1863.

SIR: Your note, forwarding a copy of Mr. Ould's letter of the 18th instant, addressed to yourself as an answer to my letter of the 13th, has been received. Mr. Ould, I perceive, states that our prisoners in Richmond receive the same rations as soldiers in the field, "according to the regulations."

The "regulations" may be such as Mr. Ould states them to be, but that our prisoners receive the "rations" as stated is contradicted by all the evidence that has reached me outside of Mr. Ould's statement; and this evidence rests upon the statements of eye-witnesses, and of actual sufferers under the treatment received in Richmond and at Belle Isle, besides the testimony of facts disclosed by the visible condition of a delivery of some one hundred and eighty prisoners made at City Point, many of whom died before reaching Fort Monroe from *starvation*, according to the judgment of a competent medical officer.

Upon the evidence above stated, the Secretary of War ordered supplies to be sent for distribution to the remaining prisoners; and this state of things induced the letter of the 13th instant, proposing to receive on parole the prisoners, and to hold them off duty until exchanged, independently of all existing difficulties on the subject of exchange.

Mr. Ould declines this offer, and proposes that if we will send to the south the prisoners in our hands they will send ours to us, "the excess on one side or the other to be on parole."

Whatever appearance of verbal fairness there may be in this, the conduct of Mr. Ould, in connexion with recent declarations of exchange, will not permit us to regard this proposal as made in good faith, and we cannot rely upon its being carried out by the enemy.

In the first place, the proclamation of Mr. Davis, and other public acts of those in power in the south, remain in full force, so far as we know, and are actually being enforced in the south, by which a distinction is made between classes of troops employed by the United States, and officers serving with colored troops, if taken prisoners, do not receive, and are not to receive, the treatment due to prisoners of war, whilst the enlisted men of colored troops, when taken prisoners, it has been publicly declared, shall be sold into slavery. That this distinction is made actual in the treatment of prisoners of war we know in some cases, and have much reason to apprehend it in others which have not been permitted to see the light.

We have positive information of the fact that two colored seamen of the United States marines were captured near Charleston and were not treated as prisoners of war. Two free colored young men, with a Massachusetts regiment, were captured near Galveston and publicly sold into slavery.

In a recent case I made a proposal to release mutually all chaplains, and the proposal was "cordially accepted;" but although we delivered about or more than twice the number we received, the enemy held back the chaplain of a Massachusetts colored regiment, who was confined and in irons at Columbia, South Carolina. In addition to these facts, Mr. Ould, not long since, declared that he would proceed to make declarations of exchange whenever he conscientiously felt that he had the right so to do, for the purpose of putting men into the field.

If this announcement means anything at all, it means that the usages of war, and the express provisions of the cartel, are subordinate to the individual determination and purposes of Mr Ould on the subject of declarations of exchanges; and, as a consequence, we must suppose that if Mr. Ould can obtain possession of the "excess" of prisoners now in our possession, he will "proceed" to declare them exchanged, and put them into the field upon what he might allege as his sense of right. When called upon for an explanation, he would prepare what he might call a "tabular statement of paroles," as he recently did, made up from guerilla captures of citizens in remote parts of the country, set down as captured at such places as Kentucky, as Tennessee, as Mississippi, as at such a place as Kentucky and Tennessee, not in any instance properly reporting to whom delivered.

Mr. Ould has shown the latitudinarian construction he puts upon his powers, and the nature of his sense of *right*, by writing a letter on the 10th October, which he has not thought it necessary to communicate to us, but which has been published in a Richmond paper, by which he took upon himself the power to declare that the whole number of men delivered by General Banks at Mobile, embracing several thousand men captured at Port Hudson, were under no obligation to observe their parole.

Mr. Ould has been a mere agent under the cartel, and when a question comes up as to the import of the cartel, its meaning, &c., Mr. Ould has no power to decide the question, for that belongs to the parties by whose authority the cartel was made.

The cartel provided two places for the delivery of prisoners of war—City Point and Vicksburg; but it provided, also, that when these places, or either of them, should become unavailable by the exigencies of war, some other point might be agreed upon.

Vicksburg having fallen into our hands became unavailable, as contemplated by the cartel; and General Banks agreed with the rebel commander in the field that General Banks would deliver the Port Hudson prisoners on parole, and they were delivered accordingly. Mr. Ould knew that those men were unconditionally in the hands of General Banks. They had been "reduced to possession," and had been taken to New Orleans, and might have been sent north if General Banks pleased. Instead of sending them to the north to swell the number of prisoners of war in our hands at the north, General Banks confided in the honor of, a rebel commander, and "agreed" to parole these men at Mobile, Vicksburg being by the exigencies of war no longer available as a place of delivery.

In that state of things Mr. Ould takes upon himself to decide that the delivery at Mobile was invalid, that place not being named in the cartel for the delivery of prisoners.

With a sense of right so obtuse as this act indicates, it is doing no injustice to Mr. Ould to say that we cannot confide in any pledge he would make to carry out a special agreement; and we must accordingly decline to acquiesce in any measure which would throw into his hands a large body of prisoners of war under parole, to be by him released from its obligations according to his sense of right.

You will understand from the above statement that Mr. Ould's decision touching the prisoners delivered by General Banks is not recognized as justifiable or valid, and that we claim that they are still prisoners of war on parole.

Very respectfully, your obedient servant,
E. A. HITCHCOCK,
Major General Vols., Comm'r for Exchange of Prisoners.
Brigadier General S. A. MEREDITH,
Commissioner for Exchange of Prisoners.

WASHINGTON CITY, D. C., *November* 28, 1863.

SIR: I have read the copy you forwarded of Mr. Ould's communication of the 21st instant, in which, I perceive, Mr. Ould thinks I misapprehend his purpose in forwarding the "tabular statement" of alleged valid paroles made chiefly in the west and south. I suppose that the tabular statement was sent to you in explanation of the large number of prisoners declared exchanged by Mr. Ould, the propriety of which had been very properly questioned by you. If that was not the purpose of the statement, I regret that it fell under my notice. If Mr. Ould wishes either to present another "statement," or to furnish detailed explanations of that already before us, it will be time enough to consider the points he may raise when he presents them. In the mean time, I think it necessary to observe that neither Mr. Ould, yourself, or myself, have powers outside of the cartel, except those plainly necessary for the execution of its provisions; but in this connexion, I must affirm that the first *shocks* given to the free and continued execution of the provisions of the cartel came from Mr. Davis in his "message" of the 12th of January, of the present year, in which he declares his purpose of delivering to the several State authorities south all commissioned officers of the federal army who might be captured, to be tried under State laws for the crime of exciting servile insurrections. This stands yet as the avowed purpose of the chief executive of the States engaged in rebellion. It has not been annulled in any form whatever; nor has the act of the southern congress in support of Mr. Davis's views been in any manner repealed or disavowed. Without looking any further, I appeal to this as a full justification of the federal commander-in-chief in suspending the operation of that portion of article 4 of the cartel, which requires all "prisoners of war to be discharged on parole in ten days after their capture;" it being manifest that the authorities south could not parole prisoners according to the cartel, and carry out their declared purpose of delivering the officers over to State authorities to be tried as *criminals* under State laws.

Whatever may have been the reason why the declared purpose of Mr. Davis has not been extensively carried into effect, the fact of the existence of that purpose, sanctioned, as we know it to have been, is a sufficient reason on our part for not delivering prisoners on parole particularly, as there is every reason to believe that the purpose of Mr. Davis has only been arrested by the fact that, by the fortune of war, we had in our hands more prisoners than were held in the south. In addition to the above, the treatment of colored troops, (which make an integral portion of the federal army,) when captured in the south, is too well known to permit us for a moment to suppose in the present state of things that there is any design in the south to treat that class of troops according to the laws of war applicable to other troops of the federal army; and until the southern authorities make some distinct declaration of a purpose to treat colored troops and their officers in the employment of the United States government in all respects according to the laws of war, as applicable to other troops, we cannot recede from the position taken by the commander-in-chief above referred to. The wisdom and the necessity of existing orders on this subject will sufficiently defend the measure in view of the *threats* and *practices* of the south, which only need to be known to justify this measure.

It is very well known that Colonel Ludlow made these subjects the frequent topic of conversation with Mr. Ould, without producing any impression on Mr. Ould, tending to the point of inducing a declaration by authority from the south that all officers of the federal army, as well as enlisted men, shall receive, when captured, the treatment due to prisoners of war, with the express declaration that colored troops, both officers and men, shall receive similar treatment.

You will please communicate these views to Mr. Ould, with a request that he will lay them before his government.

Very respectfully, your obedient servant,

E. A. HITCHCOCK,
Major General Vols., Comm'r for Exchange of Prisoners.
Brigadier General S. A. MEREDITH,
Commissioner for Exchange of Prisoners.

HEADQUARTERS 18TH ARMY CORPS,
DEPARTMENT OF VIRGINIA AND NORTH CAROLINA,
Fortress Monroe, December 17, 1863.

GENERAL: You are instructed to take charge of the matter of exchange of prisoners at City Point, and the prisoners at Point Lookout, Fort McHenry, and at Fort Norfolk, are put under your charge for that purpose, and such others will be sent you from time to time, upon notification to the War Department, as may be thought advisable.

You are herein instructed not to make any exchange which shall not return to you, man for man, officer for officer of equal rank, with those paroled and sent forward by yourself, regarding, of course, for motives of humanity, in the earlier exchanges of those officers and men, on either side, who have been the longest confined.

Colored troops and their officers will be put upon an equality in making exchanges, as of right, with other troops.

Colored men in civil employment, captured by the enemy, may also be exchanged for other men in civil employment taken by our forces.

You are permitted, in conducting the exchange, to waive for the present the consideration of the questions of parole and excess now pending between the confederate belligerent authorities and this government, leaving them untouched as they stand, until further interchange of views between those authorities and yourself.

In conducting this delicate and, perhaps, difficult matter, you will see to it that in no degree the protection of the government is withdrawn from colored soldiers of the United States and the officers commanding them, and that, in no respect, so far as results from your action, the honor or dignity of the government shall be compromised.

Brigadier General Meredith is ordered to report to you, and will be relieved from further duty as commissioner of exchange, except under your orders.

The conduct of the flag of truce, and the necessary transportation to carry out these instructions, are placed at your disposal.

You will report, as often as practicable, to this department your action under this letter of instruction and for further instruction,

By order of the Secretary of War.
E. A. HITCHCOCK,
Major General of Volunteers and Comm'r for Exchange of Prisoners.

A true copy.
E. A. HITCHCOCK,
Major General of Volunteers.

WAR DEPARTMENT,
Washington City, December 16, 1863.

GENERAL: You will proceed immediately to Fortress Monroe, and take any measure that may be practicable for the release, exchange, or relief of United States officers and soldiers held as prisoners by the rebels.

You are authorized and directed to confer with Major General Butler on the subject, and may authorize him, as special agent, commissioner, or otherwise, to procure their release or exchange upon any just terms not conflicting with principles on which the department has heretofore acted in reference to the exchange of colored troops and their officers, and not surrendering to the rebels any prisoners without just equivalents. You may, if you deem it proper, relieve General Meredith, and direct him to report to the Adjutant General for orders.

Yours, truly,
EDWIN M. STANTON,
Secretary of War.
Major General HITCHCOCK,
Commissioner of Exchange of Prisoners.

A true copy.
E. A. HITCHCOCK,
Major General of Volunteers.

General Orders, } WAR DEPARTMENT, ADJUTANT GENERAL'S OFFICE,
No. 142. } *Washington, September 25, 1862.*

The following is the cartel under which prisoners are exchanged in the existing war with the southern States:

HAXALL'S LANDING, ON JAMES RIVER, VA.,
July 22, 1862.

The undersigned, having been commissioned by the authorities they respectively represent to make arrangements for a general exchange of prisoners of war, have agreed to the following articles:

ART. 1. It is hereby agreed and stipulated that all prisoners of war held by either party, including those taken on private armed vessels known as privateers, shall be discharged upon the conditions and terms following:

Prisoners to be exchanged man for man and officer for officer; privateers to be placed upon the footing of officers and men of the navy.

Men and officers of lower grades may be exchanged for officers of a higher grade, and men and officers of different services may be exchanged according to the following scale of equivalents:

A general commanding in chief or an admiral shall be exchanged for officers of equal rank, or for sixty privates or common seamen.

A flag officer or major general shall be exchanged for officers of equal rank, or for forty privates or common seamen.

A commodore carrying a broad pennant or a brigadier general shall be exchanged for officers of equal rank, or twenty privates or common seamen.

A captain in the navy or a colonel shall be exchanged for officers of equal rank, or for fifteen privates or common seamen.

A lieutenant colonel or a commander in the navy shall be exchanged for officers of equal rank, or for ten privates or common seamen.

A lieutenant commander or a major shall be exchanged for officers of equal rank, or eight privates or common seamen.

A lieutenant or a master in the navy or a captain in the army or marines shall be exchanged for officers of equal rank, or six privates or common seamen.

Master's mates in the navy or lieutenants and ensigns in the army shall be exchanged for officers of equal rank, or four privates or common seamen.

Midshipmen, warrant officers in the navy, masters of merchant vessels, and commanders of privateers, shall be exchanged for officers of equal rank, or three privates or common seamen.

Second captains, lieutenants, or mates of merchant vessels or privateers, and all petty officers in the navy, and all non-commissioned officers in the army or marines, shall be severally exchanged for persons of equal rank, or for two privates or common seamen; and private soldiers or common seamen shall be exchanged for each other, man for man.

ART. 2. Local, State, civil, and militia rank, held by persons not in actual military service, will not be recognized, the basis of exchange being the grade actually held in the naval and military service of the respective parties.

ART. 3. If citizens held by either party on charges of disloyalty or any alleged civil offence are exchanged, it shall only be for citizens. Captured sutlers, teamsters, and all civilians in the actual service of either party, to be exchanged for persons in similar position.

ART. 4. All prisoners of war to be discharged on parole in ten days after their capture, and the prisoners now held and those hereafter taken to be transported to the points mutually agreed upon, at the expense of the capturing party. The surplus prisoners not exchanged shall not be permitted to take up arms again, nor to serve as military police or constabulary force in any fort, garrison, or field-work held by either of the respective parties, nor as guards of prisons, depots, or stores, nor to discharge any duty usually performed by soldiers, until exchanged under the provisions of this cartel. The exchange is not to be considered complete until the officer or soldier exchanged for has been actually restored to the lines to which he belongs.

ART. 5. Each party, upon the discharge of prisoners of the other party, is authorized to discharge an equal number of their own officers or men from parole, furnishing at the same time to the other party a list of their prisoners discharged and of their own officers and men relieved from parole; thus enabling each party to relieve from parole such of their own officers and men as the party may choose. The lists thus mutually furnished will keep both parties advised of the true condition of the exchange of prisoners.

ART. 6. The stipulations and provisions above mentioned to be of binding obligation during the continuance of the war, it matters not which party may have the surplus of prisoners, the great principles involved being—1st. An equitable exchange of prisoners, man for man, officer for officer, or officers of higher grade exchanged for officers of lower grade, or for privates according to the scale of equivalents; 2d. That privateers and officers and men of different services may be exchanged according to the same scale of equivalents; 3d. That all prisoners, of whatever arm of service, are to be exchanged or paroled in ten days from the time of their capture, if it be practicable to transfer them to their own lines in that time; if not, as soon thereafter as practicable; 4th. That no officer, soldier, or employé, in the service of either party, is to be considered as exchanged and absolved from his parole until his equivalent has actually reached the lines of his friends; 5th. That the parole forbids the performance of field, garrison, police, or guard, or constabulary duty.

JOHN A. DIX,
Major General.
D. H. HILL,
Major General C. S. A.

SUPPLEMENTARY ARTICLES.

ART. 7. All prisoners of war now held on either side, and all prisoners hereafter taken, shall be sent with all reasonable despatch to A. M. Aikens', below Dutch gap, on the James river, Virginia, or to Vicksburg, on the Mississippi river, in the State of Mississippi, and there exchanged or paroled until such exchange can be effected, notice being previously given by each party of the number of prisoners it will send, and the time when they will be delivered at those points respectively; and in case the vicissitudes of war shall change the military relations of the places designated in this article to the contending parties so as to render the same inconvenient for the delivery and exchange of prisoners, other places, bearing as nearly as may be the present local relations of said places to the lines of said parties, shall be by mutual agreement substituted. But nothing in this article contained shall prevent the commanders of two opposing armies from exchanging prisoners or releasing them on parole from other points mutually agreed on by said commanders.

ART. 8. For the purpose of carrying into effect the foregoing articles of agreement, each party will appoint two agents, to be called agents for the exchange of prisoners of war, whose duty it shall be to communicate with each other by correspondence and otherwise, to prepare the lists of prisoners, to attend to the delivery of the prisoners at the places agreed on, and to carry out promptly, effectually, and in good faith, all the details and provisions of the said articles of agreement.

ART. 9. And in case any misunderstanding shall arise in regard to any clause or stipulation in the foregoing articles, it is mutually agreed that such misunderstanding shall not interrupt the release of prisoners on parole, as herein.

provided, but shall be made the subject of friendly explanations, in order that the object of this agreement may neither be defeated nor postponed.

JOHN A. DIX,
Major General.
D. H. HILL,
Major General C. S. A.

By order of the Secretary of War.

L. THOMAS,
Adjutant General.

Official:

————— —————,
Assistant Adjutant General.

HEADQUARTERS 18TH ARMY CORPS,
DEPARTMENT OF VIRGINIA AND NORTH CAROLINA,
Fortress Monroe, December 7, 1863.

SIR: In obedience to your telegram, I enclose "the correspondence between the United States authorities and the rebel authorities on the exchange of prisoners, and the different propositions connected with that subject," so far as they have come from my office.

My reports and letter of instructions you have in the office at Washington.

I have the honor to be, very respectfully, your obedient servant,

BENJAMIN F. BUTLER,
Major General, Commanding.

Hon. EDWIN M. STANTON,
Secretary of War.

HEADQUARTERS 18TH ARMY CORPS,
DEPARTMENT OF VIRGINIA AND NORTH CAROLINA,
Fortress Monroe, February 2, 1862.

SIR: I have been informed that the small-pox has, unfortunately, broken out among the prisoner of war now in the hands of the confederate authorities, both at Belle Isle and at Lynchburg. Anxious, from obvious humane considerations, to prevent the spread of this terrible disorder, I have taken leave to forward for their use, by Major Mulford, assistant agent of exchange, in behalf of the United States, a package of vaccine matter, sufficient, as my medical director informs me, to vaccinate six thousand persons. May I ask that it shall be applied, under the direction of the proper medical officers, to the use intended.

Being uncertain how far I can interfere as a matter of official duty, I beg you to consider this note either official or unofficial, as may best serve the purpose of alleviating the distresses of these unfortunate men. Since learning the fact, I have had no opportunity to apply to the department at Washington for instructions. No formal receipt is needed; a note acknowledging the receipt of this being all that can be desired. If more vaccine matter is necessary it will be furnished.

I have the honor to be, very respectfully, your obedient servant,

BENJAMIN F. BUTLER,
Major General, Commanding.

Hon. ROBERT OULD,
Agent of Exchange.

Official copy:

H. C. CLARKE,
Captain and Aide-de-Camp.

CONFEDERATE STATES OF AMERICA,
War Department, Richmond, Virginia, December 9, 1863.

SIR: The package of vaccine matter has been received, and will be faithfully devoted to the purposes indicated in your letter.

Permit me, in response to the friendly tone of your letter, to assure you that it is my most anxious desire, and will be my constant effort, to do everything in my power to alleviate the miseries that spring out of this terrible war.

I have the honor to be, very respectfully, your obedient servant,
ROBERT OULD,
Agent of Exchange.

Major General B. F. BUTLER.

Official copy:

A. F. PUFFER,
Captain and Aide-de-Camp.

HEADQUARTERS 18TH ARMY CORPS,
DEPARTMENT OF VIRGINIA AND NORTH CAROLINA,
Fortress Monroe, December 25, 1864.

SIR: I have the honor to enclose to you an official copy of the authority conferring upon me the duties of commissioner of exchange of prisoners, so that we may be able to establish official relations upon that subject.

I have the honor to be, very respectfully, your obedient servant,
BENJAMIN F. BUTLER
Major General and Commissioner of Exchange.

Hon. ROBERT OULD,
Commissioner of Exchange of the Confederate Authorities.

Official copy:

H. C. CLARKE,
Captain and Aide-de-Camp.

OFFICE OF COMMISSIONER FOR EXCHANGE,
Fort Monroe, December 17, 1863.

SIR: By the authority and orders of the Secretary of War, you are hereby appointed special agent for exchange of prisoners of war, at City Point, for the purpose of executing the instructions from the War Office, of this date, addressed to you.

I have the honor to be, very respectfully, your obedient servant,
E. A. HITCHCOCK,
Major General Volunteers, Comm'r for Exchange of Prisoners.

Major General B. F. BUTLER,
Commanding, &c., Fort Monroe.

Official:

A. F. PUFFER,
Captain and Aide-de-Camp.

HEADQUARTERS 18TH ARMY CORPS,
DEPARTMENT OF VIRGINIA AND NORTH CAROLINA,
Fortress Monroe, December 25, 1863.

SIR: I send by Major Mulford, assistant commissioner of exchange, (502) five hundred and two prisoners of war, from the confederate army, from Point Lookout—all, I believe, serviceable men, and substantially those longest there in confinement.

I offer them for delivery at City Point, upon condition of receiving the same number of men held by your authorities as prisoners of war, from our army, leaving all questions of difference in controversy between your authorities and my government, for the present, in abeyance.

I have made personal examination of the condition of the prisoners of war of the confederate army, now in prison at Point Lookout, and beg leave to assure you that they are as well cared for, and in as good health, and as well fed, as the soldiers in our army.

I will send you in my next communication the statement of the sergeants, confederate prisoners, who have charge of the several cook-houses, upon that subject.

I do not mean to say that their ration is as large as our regularly issued ration, because of their state of entire inactivity, but it is in every respect of the same quality as those issued to the men generally.

If you have any doubt of it, upon an examination of the condition of the men I send you, and upon hearing their statements, please suggest what, in your judgment, should be done further in their behalf.

I have made this examination, and this statement to you, in order that you may be able to satisfy the friends of the prisoners, who may be disturbed by the unfounded reports of ill treatment and cruelty suffered by the prisoners at Point Lookout, in like manner as our people are excited by what I hope are like groundless stories of ill usage and starvation suffered by our soldiers in your hands.

I find there some of the wounded from Gettysburg, and some that have been sick that are convalescent, and some so far disabled by sickness that while they may be sent forward for exchange, they will probably be of no further service in the field.

Men without arms and legs, and debilitated by sickness, are certainly unfit to bear the necessary hardships incident to a condition of prisoners of war; besides, they encumber our hospitals.

As, upon examination, I did not think it proper to order them into the prisoners' camp, with wounds freshly healed, and health hardly restored, and as perhaps the hope of seeing their friends might have a beneficial influence upon their health, therefore I suggest that in the next transport I send up as many of these as are entirely able to bear the exposures of travelling, without probable danger to their health, and that in exchange you will return to me an equal number of our soldiers that may be in like condition. As it may be inconvenient and prejudicial to their health to tranship these invalids, on either side, I will have them put upon a separate boat, upon which there shall be nothing but provisions for them, and will direct that that boat be put at your disposal at City Point, to carry them immediately to Richmond, and bring back those that you shall give in exchange.

Of course, you will transfer, if you think best, the master and crew of the boat to the steamer New York, which will accompany them, and will remain at City Point, and put your own master and crew on board until the boat is returned.

I need not suggest the necessity of care that the boat, which is but a hired transport, shall receive no damage while in your charge, for which my government will be responsible.

And I further suggest whether the same means of avoiding transhipment might not be a convenience and facility in making further exchanges of well men, as well as invalids.

I also send four officers, lately captured at Charles City Court House, and a surgeon : one in exchange for Captain Irving, who was sent down by last boat; one at his urgent request, being suffering from injuries ; and two others, for whom you will forward me any officers of equal rank. I send these, though lately captured, because I have no officers short of Johnson's island, and I wish to avoid delay.

I also send others, prisoners whom I understand were exchanged long since, but by some oversight were not forwarded until now.

I trust such oversight will never happen again.

I have the honor to be, very respectfully, your obedient servant,
BENJAMIN F. BUTLER,
Major General Commanding, Commissioner of Exchange.
Hon. ROBERT OULD,
Commissioner of Exchange of the Confederate authorities.

Official :

A. F. PUFFER,
Captain and A. D. C.

HEADQUARTERS 18TH ARMY CORPS,
DEPARTMENT OF VIRGINIA AND NORTH CAROLINA,
Fortress Monroe, December 25, 1863.

I understand that it has been proposed by you that if the officers and crew of the steamers Emily and Arrow, captured by your forces about the 16th of May, 1863, and the boats were in the service of the United States, in the quartermaster's department when captured, the officers and men would be released. I am not informed how the proposed evidence can bear upon the matter. I therefore take the liberty of sending to you to ask if such a proposition has been made, before I look for the evidence suggested, if any such exists.

I have the honor to be your obedient servant,
BENJAMIN F. BUTLER,
Major General, Commanding.
Hon. ROBERT OULD,
Commissioner of Exchange, Richmond.

Official copy :

H. C. CLARKE,
Captain and Aide-de-Camp.

HEADQUARTERS 18TH ARMY CORPS,
DEPARTMENT OF VIRGINIA AND NORTH CAROLINA,
Fortress Monroe, December 25, 1863.

I beg leave to submit for your consideration the papers in the case of two Ohio prisoners now in the hands of the confederate authorities—Lieutenant E. H. Mason, company "D," 21st Ohio volunteers, and private John Wollam, company "E," 33d Ohio volunteers. Do me the favor to report where they are, in what condition, and if they cannot be exchanged, the reasons that lead

to that conclusion. Allow me to remark, that I do not share in the apprehension expressed by the agent of Ohio, that any wrong has or will be done them.
Please return the papers with your communication.
I have the honor to be your obedient servant,

BENJAMIN F. BUTLER,
Major General Commanding and Com'r of Exchange.

Hon. ROBERT OULD,
Commissioner of Exchange, Richmond.

Official copy:

H. C. CLARKE,
Captain and Aide-de-Camp.

HEADQUARTERS 18TH ARMY CORPS,
DEPARTMENT OF VIRGINIA AND NORTH CAROLINA,
Fortress Monroe, December 25, 1863.

The agents of the sanitary commission claim that a Mr. Alfred F. Bengle, now confined at Castle Thunder, near Richmond, was employed in the sanitary commission at the time of his arrest, was entirely non-combatant, and ought therefore to be exchanged.

I am informed that it has been proposed to exchange him for a Mr. Thatcher, also a non-combatant. We have no record of such a Mr. Thatcher. We should be willing to exchange Mr. Thatcher for Mr. Bengle, if he stands in similar circumstances. Will you give us means of making inquiry for Mr. Thatcher? Will you also forward Mr. Bengle, either conditionally or unconditionally? If we can find Mr. Thatcher, and he wishes to be exchanged, I will send him forward.

I have the honor to be,

BENJAMIN F. BUTLER,
Major General Commanding and Com'r of Exchange.

Hon. ROBERT OULD,
Commissioner of Exchange, Richmond.

Official copy:

H. C. CLARKE,
Captain and Aide-de-Camp.

CONFEDERATE STATES OF AMERICA,
War Department, Richmond, Virginia, December 27, 1863.

SIR: I have received your letter announcing your arrival with confederate prisoners. I have this day forwarded to you an equal or greater number of federal prisoners.

I received with your letter several communications from Major General Butler. In no one of them is it stated that the United States government is willing to resume the cartel and deliver all of our prisoners now in captivity, the excess on either side to be on parole. I have, more than once, expressed the entire willingness of the confederate government to deliver the federal prisoners now in our hands, provided the United States authorities will deliver the confederate prisoners in their hands. This is the provision of the cartel, and we can accept nothing less. Unless this is the distinct understanding, no equivalent will be delivered to you for any confederate officers and soldiers whom you may hereafter bring to City Point. In the hope that such is the understanding, I have directed that a number greater than the total of your delivery shall be sent to you.

In no event can we consent that the general release of prisoners so distinctly required by the cartel shall be evaded by partial deliveries. Accepting the present delivery as a step towards a general exchange on the principles of the cartel, I trust I may be permitted the hope that deliveries on the basis above indicated will be continued until all the troops in confinement on both sides are released.

Respectfully, your obedient servant,

ROBERT OULD,
Agent of Exchange.

Major JOHN E. MULFORD,
Assistant Agent of Exchange.

Official copy:

A. F. PUFFER,
Captain and Aide-de-Camp.

CONFEDERATE STATES OF AMERICA,
War Department, Richmond, Virginia, December 27, 1863.

SIR: I have this day received from Major General B. F. Butler a copy of a communication to him, signed by yourself as commissioner for the exchange of prisoners, in which it is stated that, by the authority and orders of the United States Secretary of War, Major General B. F. Butler was appointed special agent for the exchange of prisoners at City Point.

You are doubtless aware that, by proclamation of the President of the Confederate States, Major General B F. Butler is under the law of outlawry. Although we do not pretend to prescribe what agents your government shall employ in connexion with the cartel, yet, when one who has been proclaimed to be so obnoxious as General Butler is selected, self-respect requires that the confederate authorities should refuse to treat with him, or establish such relations with him as properly pertain to an agent of exchange.

The proclamation of President Davis forbids that General Butler should be admitted to the protection of the confederate government, and he cannot, therefore, be received under a flag of truce.

Accordingly, I am directed by the confederate authorities to inform you that Major General B. F. Butler will not be recognized by them as an agent of exchange.

Respectfully, your obedient servant,

ROBERT OULD,
Agent of Exchange.

Major General E. A. HITCHCOCK,
Commissioner of Exchange.

Official copy:

A. F. PUFFER,
Captain and Aide-de-Camp.

HEADQUARTERS DEPARTMENT OF VIRGINIA AND NORTH CAROLINA,
Fort Monroe, Virginia, January 12, 1864.

SIR: Your note addressed to Major General Hitchcock, in relation to the appointment by the government of the United States of a commissioner of exchange, is returned.

This government claims and exercises the power of appointing its own agents to represent its interests, irrespective of any supposed sanction by the confederate authorities.

No right of declaration of outlawry by those authorities of any officer or soldier of the United States can be admitted, or for a moment regarded by the government of the United States, as it certainly will not be by the persons upon whom such intimidation is attempted.

I am instructed to renew the offer, leaving all other questions in abeyance, to exchange man for man and officer for officer of equal rank actually held in custody by either party, until all prisoners of war so held are thus exchanged. I take leave to express the hope, from humane considerations, to those confined as prisoners of war on either side, that this offer will be accepted.

I am further instructed to inform you, that unless the flag of truce sent forward, under the sanction of the commanding general of this department, is recognized and respected by your authorities, all further communication between this government and the confederate authorities by flag of truce must cease, however much the loss of its ameliorating influences upon the rigors of what ought to be a civilized warfare is to be regretted; but the responsibility of such determination must be left with those whom you represent.

I have the honor to be, very respectfully, your obedient servant,

BENJAMIN F. BUTLER,
Major General Commanding and Commissioner of Exchange.

Hon. ROBERT OULD,
Commissioner of Exchange, Richmond, Virginia.

Official copy:

J. W. SHAFFER,
Colonel and Chief of Staff.

HEADQUARTERS DEPARTMENT OF VIRGINIA AND NORTH CAROLINA,
Fort Monroe, Virginia, January 12, 1864.

SIR: It is desirable that a list of all the prisoners held by either belligerents, whether officers or soldiers, should be furnished to each office of exchange, and also a list of all who have died on either side while held as prisoners of war.

It is also desirable that an arrangement should be made by which monthly lists shall be forwarded, as soon as practicable, up to the first of each month, of the persons captured and who have died on both sides.

I am prepared to send forward a list up to the 1st day of December, 1863, and to continue so to furnish, upon condition that you will do the same, monthly lists of prisoners and deaths as above suggested.

I beg to call to your attention that your lists already furnished contain the names of only some one hundred and twenty-three deaths. Would we could hope that list is correct, but it is impossible.

Please see to it, if this arrangement is made, that we have accurate lists of all the deaths in all the prisons and prisoners' camps wherein our officers or men are held by your authorities, and on our part it is stipulated that the utmost pains shall be taken to make like accurate lists of the officers and men, both living and dead, who are and have been held by us.

I have the honor to be, very respectfully, your obedient servant,

BENJAMIN F. BUTLER,
Major General Commanding and Commissioner for Exchange.

Hon. ROBERT OULD,
Commissioner of Exchange, Richmond, Virginia.

Official copy:

A. F. PUFFER,
Captain and Aide-de-Camp

HEADQUARTERS DEPARTMENT OF VIRGINIA AND NORTH CAROLINA,
Fort Monroe, Virginia, January 12, 1864.

SIR: It is reported that you have stipulated, if evidence is produced that the officers and crew of the steamers "Emily" and "Arrow," captured about May 5, 1863, were in the employ of the quartermaster's department when captured, the officers and men can be released from close confinement, in which we are informed they are, and treated as other prisoners of war.

I enclose the evidence of the fact for your information, and respectfully ask that you will inform me if the officers and crews of such boats can or are to be treated as prisoners of war.

I have the honor to be, very respectfully, your obedient servant,
BENJAMIN F. BUTLER,
Major General Commanding and Commissioner of Exchange.

Hon. ROBERT OULD,
Commissioner of Exchange, Richmond, Virginia.

Official copy:

A. F. PUFFER,
Captain and Aide-de-Camp.

HEADQUARTERS DEPARTMENT OF VIRGINIA AND NORTH CAROLINA,
Fort Monroe, Virginia, January 12, 1864.

SIR: In compliance with previous arrangements fifteen (15) civilians are sent up for exchange for a like number of civilians held as prisoners by your authorities.

Please receive them, and return the men for whom they are sent forward.

I have the honor to be, very respectfully, your obedient servant,
BENJAMIN F. BUTLER,
Major General Commanding and Commissioner for Exchange.

Hon. ROBERT OULD,
Commissioner of Exchange, Richmond, Virginia.

Official copy:

A. F. PUFFER,
Captain and Aide-de-Camp.

HEADQUARTERS DEPARTMENT OF VIRGINIA AND NORTH CAROLINA,
Fort Monroe, Virginia, January 12, 1864.

SIR: Enclosed please find receipt roll and certificate of thirteen (13) men claiming to be master, master's mate, and seamen in the Confederate States navy, captured at Accomac, Virginia, who were said to be in irons at Fort McHenry, and because of whose confinement certain officers and sailors of the United States navy, in the hands of your authorities, were put in irons in retaliation.

It will be seen in the certificate that they have been received by me at Fort Norfolk, and are therein treated as prisoners of war, and are not in irons. One of the men, captured at the same time, made his escape from Fort McHenry.

Ex. Doc. 17——6

I need not call your attention to the necessity of striking off the irons from those men whom you hold thus in retaliation.

Please advise me that it is so done, that I may inform the friends of the prisoners.

I have the honor to be, very respectfully, your obedient servant,

BENJAMIN F. BUTLER,
Major General Commanding and Commissioner for Exchange.

Hon. ROBERT OULD,
Commissioner of Exchange, Richmond, Virginia.

Official:

A. F. PUFFER,
Captain and Aide-de-Camp.